# The Country Writer's Craft

Writing for Country, Regional
and Rural Publications

# The Country Writer's Craft

Writing for Country, Regional
and Rural Publications

Suzanne Ruthven

**COMPASS
BOOKS**

Winchester, UK
Washington, USA

First published by Compass Books, 2013
Compass Books is an imprint of John Hunt Publishing Ltd., Laurel House, Station Approach,
Alresford, Hants, SO24 9JH, UK
office1@jhpbooks.net
www.johnhuntpublishing.com
www.compass-books.net

For distributor details and how to order please visit the 'Ordering' section on our website.

Text copyright: Suzanne Ruthven 2012

ISBN: 978 1 78279 001 3

A CIP catalogue record for this book is available from the British Library.

Design: Stuart Davies

Printed and bound by CPI Group (UK) Ltd, Croydon, CR0 4YY

We operate a distinctive and ethical publishing philosophy in all
areas of our business, from our global network of authors to
production and worldwide distribution.

# CONTENTS

# Introduction

My first introduction to the skill of writing for country publications came from the pen of legendary Ian Niall of *Country Life*, who for forty years contributed the weekly 'Countryman's Notes' to the magazine, and during that time acquired a devoted readership that spanned the world.

Secondly, and by no means least, the inimitable Willy Poole's regular columns in the *Sunday Telegraph, Daily Mail, Telegraph Weekend Magazine, Daily Express, Mail on Sunday, Horse & Hound...* that were always irreverent, witty and *completely* non-PC. A few years ago, I had the pleasure to meet 'my hero' at the Peterborough Festival of Hunting and found him utterly delightful and completely up to expectations!

Unfortunately, the countryside of Ian Niall and Willy Poole no longer exists and those who write about it (with the exception of the irascible Robin Page) are, more often than not, folk who can never really lay claim to being 'country born and bred' in the true sense. Even the traditional nuances of county writing have altered and, as a result, those who want to write for country, regional or rural publications must pay strict attention to the submission guidelines of each one, since editorial requirements can also alter drastically from one magazine to another.

There is one hard and fast rule, however, that no editor can change, and that is the fact that *all* country writing remains seasonal-based. This means that the writer often needs to submit material 6–12 months in advance of the publication for which it is intended. It is pointless glancing out of the window and thinking that the pleasant scene of rolling cornfields might spark off an idea – because you've already missed the deadline! Write the article by all means, but it won't see publication until a year hence. That is why this how-to book is set out month-by-month, and not in the usual chapter-by-chapter format, together with examples of material that has already seen the light of day in various country publications for guidance.

Suzanne Ruthven

Glen of Aherlow – 2013

Suzanne Ruthven has written on country topics for over 30 years, and as well as being published in *The Countryman* and *Country Illustrated*, she is author of *A Treasury of the Countryside, Champagne & Slippers, Hearth & Garden, Life-Writes* and *Signposts For Country Living*. She is also commissioning editor for Compass Books, the writers' resource imprint for John Hunt Publishing. *www.johnhuntpublishing.com/facebook.com/JHPCompassBooks*

# January: The Dark Month

Most people enjoy reading about countryside, regional or rural affairs, and whereas women are acknowledged to be the readers of the majority of mainstream weekly and monthly publications, country magazines can also lay claim to having a large male readership. Surprisingly, many of these magazines refuse to publish anything to do with 'hunting, shooting and fishing', while others are devoted to this aspect of living and working in the countryside. Farming publications are mainly concerned with the day to day requirements of earning a living off the land; smallholders are catered for with the more modest approach to a rural existence. Regional magazines reflect the lifestyle of the more rural parts of the counties or regions, while rural publications (including parish magazines and free papers) will be more interested in community-oriented matters and entertainment.

If we are only interested in writing for one small area of this genre, then our marketplace is going to be extremely limited indeed – so we are going to have to learn to think outside the box and find original ways to interest an editor. In other words, when we intend to write in a specialised genre, **we have to think like a professional writer**.

Professionalism isn't just about making sure there aren't too many typos in our article, or submitting a beautifully presented typescript. It's about attitude – gaining experience, knowledge and understanding of the publishing world – and that takes time and effort to acquire. The PW (Professional Writer) understands that the entire publishing industry needs to be mentally boiled down into four categories – probables, possibles, highly-unlikelies and the definitely-nots. He or she never dismisses an outlet, however, until their minds have explored all the permutation, but neither do they overestimate their own worth.

The PW's credits tell the editor all they want to know; and a poem published in the *Bondage & Latex Users Weekly* is unlikely to impress a commissioning editor at *The Shooting Times*. The PW merely lists those publication credits relevant to his/her current mission. The typescripts are word-counted, double-spaced and easy to read because the PW knows that an editor's eye is trained to speed-read at approximately 250 words to the page. The PW will always be scanning the reshuffle of magazine ownership and changes of editor, and be quick to pick up on the shift of trends in an editorial approach to field sports.

The PW also knows that magazines on the newsagent's shelves only reflect the 'popular' end of the market, and want to know which new columnists are considered to be the next generation of up-and-coming country writers. New editors can mean drastic changes for magazine features and the PW doesn't consider *any* publication as out-of-bounds.

A word of warning – editors, like elephants, have hellishly long memories. One editor within country publishing has, over the years, edited four different magazines. In the early days, he was subjected to a series of abusive and insulting letters from a would-be contributor. The editor is still receiving submissions from his old enemy and point-blank refuses to even read the contents. "It still gives me a great feeling of pleasure to write, *'not suitable for this publication'* across the rejection slip," he confessed.

Professional writers are, of course, a joy to work with since they understand that freelance writing is a buyer's market – and the editor/publisher is the one with all the choice. Having familiarised themselves with a publication, PWs will often e-mail or phone with an idea, only to have the editor reject it – but pick up on other points that have been raised and suggest these as an alternative feature. This is a common occurrence when, during the exchange, the freelance lets slip a previously unmentioned item which is a hundred times more exciting than the original proposal. The editor's favourites are the ones who can set out a concise letter of introduction, a detailed outline and offer something interesting to publish.

The PW rarely writes anything without first knowing where they are going to send the finished typescript, and there is little in life that is more uplifting to a writer than an e-mail of acceptance from an editor or publisher. It's what, after all, every writer aspires to when she or he turns on the computer and opens up a new file for the latest idea. **This is what Professional Writers do – they write for publication**. They do not waste time nit-picking and waffling; they get on with the job in hand. The PW doesn't have the time for any other form of writing because every hour wasted in displacement activity is an hour away from a current project or commission. So, before we begin, get an attitude – a professional one – and start understanding the market you want to write for.

## Write About What You Know – or Can Learn About

Our first task is to explore the publications in the genre, regardless of where we live in the world. Taking a leaf out of the Professional Writer's book, we should never dismiss an outlet until we have explored *all* the possibilities, and never *over*estimate our ability to write for the 'glossies' until we have some impressive credits under our collective belts.

Each magazine will represent the multitude of different country attitudes that will be encountered wherever we live, and give a simple guide on how and where the *readership* sees itself fitting into the scheme of things. And if we look closely at the following breakdown of magazines, we can immediately see that this is one of the widest marketplaces for finding outlets for our work. These are just a few of the international publications that we can target:

- For the 'bred in the bone' type of people, who see the countryside as an integral part of their lives, livelihood and heritage [i.e. *Country Life, The Field, Scottish Field, Irish*

*Countrysports & Country Life, Irish Country Magazine, Scottish Sporting Gazette, Shooting Gazette*]. **See February.**

- Farming publications that provide the farming community with the latest developments in fertilizers, foodstuffs, machinery and livestock maintenance [i.e. *Farmers Weekly, the Farmers Journal* (Ireland), *Farming Magazine* (USA), *Australian Farm Journal*]. **See March.**

- The 'glossy monthly' that features people, conservation, wildlife, cookery, rural houses and gardens, and country businesses – but rarely found in a working farmhouse kitchen [i.e. *Country Living, LandLove, Irish Country Magazine, Country Living* (USA), *Rural Living Canada*]. **See April.**

- Others maintain a rather genteel and romantic/nostalgic approach to country matters, that don't really reflect a true picture as they resolutely refuse to feature any reference to field sporting events, which are still very much an integral part of rural life [i.e. *The Countryman, This England, Country Magazine* (USA), *Australian Country Craft*]. **See May.**

- Smallholding publications give practical advice on small-scale poultry and livestock keeping (including rare breeds), country crafts, gardening and cookery. The approach is aimed at those who wish to establish a living from what they produce or rear on the land [i.e. *Country Smallholding, Practical Poultry, Smallholder, Small Farm Canada, Hobby Farm Magazine* USA, *Homesteading* (USA), *Countryside Magazine* (Australia)]. **See June.**

- 'Good Life' magazines are more 'kitchen table' than 'coffee table' and cater for those looking for a life of self-sufficiency. Directing them towards realistic solutions with practical articles tailored towards the smaller acreage [i.e. *Home Farmer, Urban Farmer* (USA), *City Farmer* (Australia)]. **See July.**

- Regional and county magazines are usually glossy

monthly or quarterly publications featuring county events, entertainment, businesses and personality profiles of local people [i.e. *Welsh Country*, all County magazines, i.e. *Sussex Life, National Trust Magazine*]. **See August.**

- Hunting, shooting and fishing magazines have a workman-like approach to vermin control and catching food for the 'pot' or freezer [*The Countryman's Weekly, The Shooting Gazette, The Shooting Times, Fieldsports Magazine, Game and Fish Magazine* (USA), *Gray's Sporting Journal* (USA), *Outdoor Canada, Hunting & Wildlife Magazine* (NZ)]. **See September.**

- Rural publications cover local community newsletters, free newspapers and parish newsletters. **See October.**

- Equine and rural sporting magazines often provide an overlap between rural and urban readers [*Horse & Hound, Pony Club News* (USA), *Lakeland Walker, Country Walking, Hill Walking Magazine, Camping Magazine, Outsider Magazine* (Ireland), *Backpacker* (USA), *Go Camping* (Australia)]. **See November.**

- Wildlife publications have a very wide readership that often has little connection with country living but can provide another marketplace [*BBC Wildlife Magazine, Irish Wildlife Magazine, Canadian Wildlife Magazine, National Wildlife Magazine* (USA), *Wildlife Australia Magazine*]. **See December.**

- Book publishers who accept full-length typescripts on all aspects of country living. [The Good Life Press, Countryside Books, Merlin Unwin Books, Quiller Publishing, Shire Books]. **See *Once In A Blue Moon.***

Our first task will be to acquire copies of the magazines that appear to offer the best market **for our particular writing style**, together with the relevant submission guidelines. And although I can bang on about market research *ad nauseam*, it *is* one of the most important aspects of creative writing.

When we begin our writing career, the most vital lesson we *should* learn is the importance of thoroughly researching the marketplace for potential outlets. This is not merely a question of sending along something in a similar vein hoping for an acceptance; it is the continual study of a particular publication so we become familiar with that editor's preferences. It doesn't matter how competent we are with the written word, it will be of no avail if we haven't concentrated our efforts on finding out all there is to know about our target magazine.

Choose the most current issues available and read through each magazine very carefully, paying particular attention to the advertisements because these give an even clearer indication to the age/reader/market profile for that particular publication. Magazines are filled with all sorts of articles, on a vast variety of subjects, but again we need to analyse a selection of those already accepted by the editor before submitting anything of our own.

What sort of style appeals to the readers? Are the examples factual, argumentative, emotive, nostalgic, how-to? Do they offer a subject for discussion, or do they merely mirror the author's opinion? Choose six country magazines for analysis and, picking three articles from each, compare them with the following:

- Do the majority of articles contain any new information, or ideas linked with current viewpoints or issues?
- If the article covers a familiar subject, is it written from a fresh and interesting angle? If so, outline the point of interest.
- Does the title catch the eye and if so, why?
- Does the lead paragraph hold your attention and is the subject clearly introduced in the opening paragraph?
- Do the articles consist of long or short paragraphs? Do long or short words predominate? How many words to a sentence? Do the articles comprise of easy to understand

words?

- Is the house style of the publication chatty, friendly, formal or pompous?
- At what type of person are the advertisements aimed?

Research, however, does not necessarily end with the collecting of targets through market research. To add a more professional dimension to features and articles, we will need to interview people and organisations that have experience in our subject. Editors and publishers want original material that includes input from fresh sources; it is not enough to regurgitate previously published ideas; we need to think of some new ones of our own.

It is not, of course, easy to be original – after all, even the philosophers tell us that there is no such thing as original thought. As far as writing is concerned, being original means trying to find a different approach to a subject, even to portray it from another angle, play 'Devil's Advocate' and offer an alternative viewpoint. Have a look at the following previously published example of what appealed to the editor of *The Countryman* for a January issue.

## Life As It Is Lived: The Country Kitchen

Think of the country kitchens from your childhood and what images immediately spring to mind? There's usually the battered Aga (or Rayburn) of course, but more often than not, in our grandparents' house a huge black range, with its multiple ovens and a roaring fire in the grate, would dominate the kitchen in both summer and winter. The ovens were rarely used for cooking once a modern gas stove had been installed but they saved the lives of numerous lambs, kittens and chicks, as well as drying boots and airing the washing. And mingled with the heady aroma of the week's baking, there would be the underlying smell of damp leather from tack drying by the fire.

By the hearth was always a large, comfortable (if rather

grubby) armchair where grandfather, straight from the fields, could find comfort for a while without having to worry about trailing mud through grandmother's inner sanctum of cleanliness. On a small sofa, equally battered and grubby, a dog or two would be curled, only marginally cleaner than their human companion, but always alert and waiting for the next outing.

The battered furniture might have gone but in any country kitchen there is always a constant battle between mud and dogs' hair. Kitchen floors are still flagstoned or quarry tiled, since nothing else is durable enough to withstand the seasonal traipsing in of mud and muck, no matter how well we clean our boots.

Most meals are still taken at the kitchen table – often an enormous well-scrubbed pine affair that had supported countless generations of elbows during the house's long history. During the dark month of January work in the fields is kept to a minimum as the cattle and sheep are fed closer to home, and this gives neighbours the opportunity to call – their arrival timed to coincide with the latest batch of baking and the ubiquitous tea loaf. This recipe has its roots in wartime austerity and its spicy aroma regularly wafts around our kitchen today.

## RECIPE: Tea Loaf

*1 cup cold tea*
*1 egg*
*3 ozs margarine*
*1 teacup sugar*
*1 teacup mixed fruit*
*2 large cups self-raising flour*
*½ teaspoon nutmeg*
*½ teaspoon mixed spice*

Simmer the tea, margarine, sugar and fruit in a saucepan for 3 minutes and then allow to cool. Mix with flour and beaten egg and pour into a 2 lb loaf tin lined with greaseproof paper. Bake for 1 hr 20 mins on Gas Mark 4 (or 180 C).

This morning's visitors are tough local farmers, a father and daughter duo who breed terriers and horses in equal quantities here in the Glen. Both red-faced and square-set, they can only be told apart by *his* bushy side-whiskers and *her* pearl stud earrings. Booted and capped, the Battersbys have just returned from the hospital following treatment for a broken toe sustained when their tractor overturned on the ice. The vehicle was stuck fast between the high, sloping sides of the *boreen,* and if there hadn't been the confines of the cab to prevent Battersby senior from spilling out into the road, the accident would have been fatal.

Nevertheless, with an Irish relish for the near-death experience and illness, we are regaled with the story yet again, with both father and daughter talking at the same time, each anxious to deliver the punchline about God's good luck, and both tugging at slipper and sock to reveal the purple-hued extremity. The more grisly aspects of the naked foot with its horned toenails are averted by the production of a pot of coffee and the tea loaf. An hour later, all that are left are the crumbs and the Battersbys have hobbled out in unison into the biting wind, reluctant to leave the warmth of our comfortable modern kitchen to go back to the chill of their stable yard. The dogs watch them go, but make no move to escort them off the premises as is their usual custom.

With modern climate change knocking the seasons out of kilter there is, however, something reassuring about deep snow and freezing conditions around Midwinter and the New Year. We may be inconvenienced for a few days by electricity cuts and frozen pipes, but for a brief moment, we have an insight into how our ancestors viewed these conditions: huddling together for warmth around a meagre fire, with fuel and food supplies running low, and wolves prowling outside, waiting to feed off the dead. This is a mysterious frozen world where trees loom ghost-like out of the mist. Everything is covered with a glittering film of hoar-frost that forms when moisture in the air freezes on cold surfaces (usually overnight), producing ice crystals in the shape of scales, needles, feathers and fans.

There is an old country saying that a foot of snow is worth an inch of rain, simply because melting snow slowly percolates down into the subsoil. For all the disruption it causes, the thawing process is so slow that most of the water finds its way into the underground water systems, the maze of streams flowing along the underworld of the land. These extremes of winter weather are Nature's way of demonstrating that, despite all the scientific advancement, humans have little control over their life on the planet.

January is the month when all seems to be stillness and silence. Small animals remain hidden, hibernating, or sleeping to conserve energy. Migrant birds left in the autumn and it will be many months before they return. Insects are dead or dormant. The fields seem empty but even in these freezing conditions the delicate green shoots of the woodbine, or wild honey-suckle can be detected in the hedgerow at the bottom of the kitchen garden. The weak winter sun reflects on the bright yellow flowers of a sheltered gorse bushes, even if the blossoms are seared by frost.

In the dark month of January there is little available by way of 'wild food' for use in our country kitchen. If the frost hasn't been too severe, we may be lucky enough to find a supply of early chickweed in the garden or field edge. This common weed can be cooked with spring onions as a fresh vegetable (simmer for 2 mins with a knob of butter), or served as a salad – and is one of the tenderest of wild green stuff, with a taste reminiscent of corn salad or a mild lettuce. We're probably more familiar with it as a healing and soothing agent, made into a decoction to wash and bathe swollen and inflamed injuries (*a la* Battersby's toe), and it's been used in this way for centuries in domestic plant medicine, being listed by Nicholas Culpeper for relieving itching skin conditions.

Traditionally, ploughing the fields in preparation for sowing was the first task of the agricultural year, and the first Monday after Twelfth Night is still known as Plough Monday. This was the day on which farmhands returned to work after the Midwinter holiday – not that any work was actually done as the day was marked by various customs and merrymaking, with mumming plays and a 'molly dance'. This year, church blessing or not, there will be no more ploughing done until the weather breaks and until then, it's the country kitchen with its roaring Aga that remains the focal centre of our smallholding.

**Published in the January 2013 issue of *The Countryman***

As you can see from this example, there is a wide blend of nostalgia, country-lore, modern farming, local characters, humour and kitchen craft – all mixed together to produce an up-to-date, full-length country kitchen feature that would appeal to a general readership. The whole piece is based on personal observances, both past and present, to create a montage of winter farmhouse kitchen images. It doesn't matter that the sequences didn't take place as one continuous observation; each occurrence happened in its own time and has been grafted together to create a cameo of real country life.

## Marketplace

The first marketplace for us to explore are the competitions that cater specifically for country or nature writers. Do bear in mind that not all competitions are annual events and so a certain amount of research is necessary – and remember that 'specialty writing' competitions do not generally draw the high number of entrants normally associated with national events, so it's worth a try.

The most well-known are the **BBC's Nature Writer of the Year**, that invites an 800-word piece of nature writing on animals, birds, plants, natural events or places, or any combination of these; plus **Travel Writer of the Year** and **Wildlife Artist of the Year**.

See http://www.discoverwildlife.com/competitions

If you are interested in entering several of the *Countryside Tales'* open competitions it may be worthwhile considering taking out an annual subscription to the magazine, which entitles you to unlimited free entry in all the events. Park Publications run several competitions every year including two open poetry competitions, two open short story competitions and the annual article competition all with a country theme. These competitions are in addition to those in each issue of the magazines. See **www.parkpublications.co.uk/countrytales.htm**

Nature has always challenged writers to write their very best and so the brief is simple: write an engaging and inspiring 2,000-word non-fiction piece celebrating/exploring the wonder of Nature and your own relationship with it for the **Resurgence & Ecologist Nature** Writing Contest. **See www.theecologist.org for more details.**

Despite the competition rules being clearly set out, it is surprising just how many entrants refuse to work within the parameters set out by the organisers. Never exceed the stated word count because if your entry is found to be 100 words too long, it *will* be disqualified – and it will be your own fault if you lose your entry fee. If the organisers have set a theme for the competition – stick to it. The selectors are instructed to look for the best interpretation of that theme, and if you've ignored it, you won't be in the running, no matter how good your entry.

One competition rule that does need some clarification was raised by the disqualification of the winning entry in a national competition. The rules for most competitions usually state that entries must be... 'original, unpublished and not entered for any current competition' – and it was subsequently discovered that the winning entry had been selected previously as the winner in a writers' group competition, and the piece published in the group's newsletter. Understandably it was thought that inclusion in a private newsletter did not count as having been 'previously published'. As far as competitions are concerned, any work appearing in printed or online form (unless otherwise stated), and no matter how modest, should be considered as 'published' – especially when it comes to competitions where large cash prizes are at stake. If in doubt, raise the question with the organisers well in advance of the closing date. Believe me, if you don't point it out, someone else will!

## Exercise: The First Steps

Select one of the above or track down a rural competition running in any of the country magazines and, following the given guidelines, prepare your entry for the current competition. Although there is either a set theme, or the subject matter is 'open', spend some time in coming up with an original approach, or a different slant on a popular topic. Where possible, study the style of previous winners of that event, and avoid stereotypical articles that don't contain a nugget of fresh information.

Or subscribe to *Countryside Tales*, launched in March 2000 by Park Publications. It is an illustrated magazine in A5 format and is published quarterly. The editor is also interested in any non-fiction with a countryside/rural theme which should be up to 1500 words on any issue related to the countryside: biographies, childhood memories, nature/wildlife etc. Short fillers of up to 400 words are also welcome. This is idyllic, reminiscent material, harping back to childhood and the loss of things past. It is a sharing of thoughts about the countryside and bygone days and contains all kinds of material about the British countryside. Illustrated with attractive line drawings, it also features short stories and poems with a countryside theme. The editor is happy to discuss ideas with writers and even expresses a willingness to offer advice on how material could be improved – an ideal introduction into writing for country magazines.

# February: The most unpleasant weather of the year

One thing that the country writer must avoid at all costs is an overly sentimental view of the rural lifestyle. We read about it being a haven of perfect calm and silence but in reality a working farm can produce a veritable cacophony of sounds and smells that can certainly rival any industrial site. Sound carries a very long way over open farmland and anyone living within three miles (as the crow flies) of a farmyard will be adversely affected by the noise from sheep, cattle and especially cockerels. Similarly, farmers begin work at 'sparrow fart' and the monotonous throb of a generator powering the milking sheds is not a recipe for inducing sleep. In the summer months there is the constant rumble of wagons through the villages well into the night if the race is on to beat the weather and get the hay, silage, straw or grain under cover.

Generally speaking, however, rural living is far less competitive and materialistic than urban people are used to, where more often than not everyone is judged by what they do and what they own. Remember that different sorts of clothes and footwear are worn in the country, and most folk tend to shop at the local branch of 'country store' rather than swanning around in designer labels. Country roads, pub car parks and gravel drives can cut the Jimmy Choos to ribbons! This is the land of shabby chic, and a battered 4X4 blends in better than the latest model Lexus – unless we're in Newmarket. That's why the country question arose: "What's the difference between a hedgehog and a Range Rover?" Answer: "On a hedgehog all the pricks are on the outside."

Also dogs have a very high profile in the country and it is not uncommon for one to be seen happily paddling through slurry or bringing home a decomposing roadkill. In fact, country dogs are often given a new Barbour to break in for their owners by using it to line the dog-basket. The reasoning behind this bizarre behaviour is because no self-respecting country person would be seen dead in a brand new one! Dogs often get a mention in country writers' articles since they are the seen as the 'constant companion', who – like his owner – is permanently damp and clogged up to his armpits in mud... and never learns to wipe his feet before sprawling on the sofa for a post-lunch snooze.

## The Study of Nature

As Stefan Buczacki observes in *Fauna Britannica*, the conservation of and caring for our fauna [and flora] has become a minor growth industry over the past 20 or 30 years, and conservationist might not necessarily agree with the way that the farming community views the countryside. And this consideration needs to be taken when writing articles for the individual country publications, especially when there is a change of editor. New editors come with all their pride and prejudices intact and if the former editor was a great field sports enthusiast, don't take it for granted that the newly appointed helmsman or woman is going to follow in his waders.

Any writer's bookshelf should have a reliable collection of natural history books that include comprehensive details about animals, birds, insects, butterflies, wild flowers and trees. These are used to confirm sightings, the correct names (Latin or local) and check habitat, not to mention the way that they have enriched our culture, serving as the origin of local and national traditions, superstitions and place names – which are all grist for the writer's mill in order to spice up an article.

We also need to be familiar with the fact that long hot summers with gentle rain produce a bumper crop of wild fruits in the hedgerows such as crab apples, sloes, elderberries, rosehips, hazelnuts, blackberries and rowan berries. All are delicious when made into flavoured vinegars, chutneys, jams and liqueurs, although wild fruits should be looked upon as accompaniments to meals rather than dishes in their own right. This is usually because they take a long time to pick and the amounts are relatively small. Most lack the high sugar levels of cultivated fruit, which makes them too bitter to use on their own, but right up until WWII most country households would have stocked up with provisions made from wild fruit.

Rowan jelly is perfect with venison or game, and crab apple 'cheese' gives an unusual edge to cold pork and cheddar cheese. Then there is blackberry kir and sloe gin. Try making your own horseradish from the wild variety, which is much better than any shop-bought concoctions. Elderberry syrup is an old Tudor remedy for winter colds, particularly when mixed with honey, hot water and a dash of whisky. There are numerous cookery books devoted to country recipes and anyone who is seriously interested in stocking up the larder from the hedgerows should invest in one. There is nothing quite like home-made preserves and there is a certain sense of satisfaction in eating produce from the wild.

Did you know, however, that you could be prosecuted for picking wild flowers? In fact all wild plants are given some protection under the laws of the United Kingdom and the Republic of Ireland. Under the Wildlife & Countryside Act 1981, which covers Britain, it is illegal to uproot any wild plant without permission from the landowner or occupier. Uproot is defined as 'to dig up or otherwise remove the plant from the land on which it is growing.' Even plants growing wild are the legal property of somebody and, for the purposes of legislation, the term 'plant' includes algae, lichens and fungi as well as true plants – mosses, liverworts and vascular plants.

Certain rare wild plants are given legal protection against deliberate picking of the flowers, collecting, cutting, uprooting and destruction, with the regulations applying to all stages in the biological cycle of listed plants such as creeping marshwort, early gentian, fen orchid, floating water-plantain, Killarney fern, lady's slipper, marsh saxifrage, shore dock and slender naiad. Lists of rare species can be obtained from the Joint Nature Conservation Committee, or viewed on its website.

But even common plants can suffer: "On the farm we have an old bluebell wood which has been there for centuries," said one farmer's wife. "It's not an uncommon site to see newcomers walking out of there with armfuls of the flowers, which they pick without asking. No country person would ever pick bluebells because they droop as soon as they've been picked and land up in the dustbin within half an hour of being pulled out from the bulbs. Why the hell can't they leave them alone?" Another neighbour remembers there being carpets of snowdrops and primroses in her local woods. "For years people moving into the area would come along in the spring and dig up the plants. Now, fifty years later, there are only a few areas where they still flower naturally."

What many people don't realise is that the British countryside has an impressive collection of highly poisonous plants that can have fatal results for the unsuspecting. Deadly nightshade, or to give it its more sinister name, *atropa belladonna*, is often found in the neighbourhood of ruins and on the sites of former gardens. The whole plant has an unpleasant smell and is generally poisonous, with the juice of the berries being especially so. These have often proved fatal to children.

Ragwort is one of the most frequent causes of livestock poisoning and results in the painful death of horses, ponies and donkeys each year. The pretty yellow flower hides a poisonous heart. It can be found in a number of places, including roadsides and motorway verges, where a single plant can produce thousands of new plants for the following season. When eaten in hay, ragwort causes irreversible liver damage. A woman was recently prosecuted and banned from keeping animals for life after she was found guilty of allowing two of her horses to eat the plant. Ragwort is also dangerous to humans and can cause severe blistering to the skin if handled without protective gloves. On the plus side (from the conservationist's point of view), the plant provides countless butterflies and insects with a food source.

There are dozens of more familiar plants such as foxgloves, daffodils and bluebells that can cause unpleasant reactions in the unsuspecting, and many more that can be fatal to cats and dogs if eaten. Invest in an illustrated book of wild flowers and make a point of studying the hedgerows near your home for the tell-tale signs of toxic plants. Unless your children are particularly precocious there is no need to dig the plants up, even if they appear in the garden; after all, many of them have been used in folk-medicine for centuries and are all part of the countryside's rich tapestry!

The British Isles also has more species of toxic fungi than anywhere else in Europe and it is not a subject that can easily be learned from books. The external characteristics of many species are very changeable and cannot always be identified with certainty. There is nothing to beat fresh, wild mushrooms, but this is not an area for the novice because some are highly toxic and can kill – others become more dangerous if eaten in conjunction with alcohol, such as *coprinus atramentarius*. Or, as one countryman said casually over a pint, "Eat half a death cap (*amanita phalloides*) and it's not a case of whether you may die, but how long it will take you to die."

It's obviously necessary to reflect these small, but important details in our articles if we hope to be taken seriously as country writers. And one of the best places to find these snippets of information is *The Penguin Guide to the Superstitions of Britain and Ireland* that will provide us with endless examples of these 'small but important details' and endless ideas for integrating rural customs and observations into our writing – as shown in the following example...

## Life As It Is Lived: Muddy Lanes and Damp Woods

February was known as the Death Moon, when the long, cold days of winter would have taken their toll in times past when food-stocks were beginning to run low – and represented by the ash tree. During the 5th century the pagan festival of Imbolc (2nd February – which celebrated the start of the Celtic lambing season) was changed to Candlemas – the feast of the Purification of the Virgin Mary, although the name of February comes from an old Roman festival 'Februa'. It was the feast day of Bride or Brigit, the goddess of the British tribe, the Brigantia, when ribbons were tied to the outside of the window to let her know she was welcome in the house.

A weather prophecy associated with this day claims:

*If Candlemas be fair and bright, winter will have another flight; but if Candlemas brings cloud and rain, winter is gone and won't come again.*

During the winter, ash trees are easily recognised by the sooty-black buds arranged in opposite pairs along the twigs. The ash – another native tree under threat from a sinister fungal disease – is the last of the trees to show its foliage and the first to lose it in the autumn. Ash wood is both supple and closely grained, resisting shock without splintering and was often used in weaponry. In Norse mythology the *ask* held an honoured place, appearing as *Askr*, the Father of Mankind. The myth claims that when the gods wanted to populate the earth they took an ash tree and breathed the human soul into it and Askr was born, while woman was fashioned from an alder tree. The ash is one of the nine sacred woods and one of the nine Celtic Chieftain Trees, and in country-lore, it is possible to predict whether we can expect a dry or wet summer:

*If the oak before the ash, we will only ha ye a splash*

*If the ash before the oak, we will have a soak*

February is the time for spectacular sunrises and sunsets for which the countryman has an in-built appreciation. For those who take the time to stand and stare, there are those few fleeting moments of a true 'Turner skyscape' when a whole kaleidoscope of colour is visible. Turner was often accused of exaggerating the colours and forms of nature but, as he was alleged to have retorted to the woman who complained that *she* never saw his skies in nature – "Then God help you, madam."

In the early morning light we can often find the 'slot marks', or hoof prints of deer in the frozen mud on the farm track. It is hard to imagine that there is a deer problem when we hardly ever see them but, as any stalker will tell you, 99 per cent of the human population lives within a mile of one type of deer or another.

Unfortunately, when deer overpopulate, disease soon kicks in and the death rate from parasites and pneumonia goes up, which is why it is important to keep the numbers at a manageable level. For the generations who have shed a tear over the shooting of Bambi's mother, the necessity for killing these beautiful creatures is a bitter pill to swallow but venison makes a pleasant change to the Sunday roast and one the countryman would look forward to with relish.

## Roast Venison

Venison is classified as game and the prime cuts are leg and loin, which are usually roasted after it has been marinated. Venison is rarely dry roasted but braised, the liquid helping to moisten the meat during cooking. The meat should be placed in a roasting tin with a mixture of fat, oil and/or wine in which it was marinated; it may also be covered with slices of streaky bacon. The meat is best roasted in an oven preheated to very hot Gas Mark 8 / 450 F / 230 C and should be basted every 20 minutes with the juices in the tin.

The traditional accompaniments to roast venison are a tart fruit sauce, made with such fruits as redcurrants or cranberries, thin gravy and vegetables. Try this 17<sup>th</sup> century recipe from Yorkshire to accompany venison or venison steaks.

### RECIPE: Old Currant Sauce

*2 oz currants*
*8 fl oz port*
*1/2 teaspoon ground cloves*
*2 slices bread (crusts removed arid made into breadcrumbs)*
*2 oz butter*

Soak the currants in the port for about an hour, then transfer fruit with the cloves added into a saucepan. Add the bread-crumbs and butter and simmer gently for about 20 minutes until the mixture thickens.

Spells of warm weather bring out the grey squirrels to forage in the dead leaves for nuts they've hidden during the autumn. Although officially classed as vermin, it's difficult not to be amused by the antics of an animal that is a natural clown and has little fear of humans. The grey squirrel, however, was only intro-duced to Britain from North America in the late 19<sup>th</sup> century and 60 per cent of them carry the *parapoxvirus*, that kills our native red squirrels within four or five days of contact.

In the ponds, sticklebacks and frogs are coming out of hibernation to find a mate. The frog gets its name from the Anglo-Saxon word *frogga* and is often still referred to by its country name of 'paddock'. Widely associated with witchcraft and super-stition, the poor old frog has often been the victim of cruel mutilation; tadpoles were once swallowed alive in the belief that they cured gout! Conversely, it is widely believed to be unlucky to kill a frog as they are said to possess the soul of a boy or girl who died in childhood. Although a more benign frog charm says that frog croaking during the day is an omen of rain, while if one comes into your house of its own accord then it is a sign of good luck to follow.

The winter heliotrope, although not a native of these shores, reaches its peak in mid-February, having attracted the early insects with its vanilla-like fragrance. Celandines bloom in the hedgerows, the yellow flowers competing with the scattered pockets of gorse that gallantly flowers throughout the year even if there is only a single spray of flowers. Thus proving the old saying: *"When the gorse is out of bloom, kissing's out of season."*

Yellow flowers also appear on the coltsfoot, a plant associated with bronchial complaints in British herbals. Coltsfoot has been widely used for many centuries, with no record of ill effects. An infusion of 2–4 g per cup can be used as a relaxing expectorant for stubborn, tight coughs, for chronic chest problems and asthma. The leaves can be used in a poultice or ointment for cuts and poorly healing wounds. In the woods, bluebells leaves are beginning to push their spikes through the dead undergrowth as wild honeysuckle sends out its shoots in an attempt to gain a head start before the woodland canopy blots out the sunlight. Fluffy yellow catkins on the hazel give the sign that this is the first deciduous tree to come alive again from its winter sleep.

Moorhens can be seen on the banks of ponds and streams foraging for frostbitten sloes and haws to supplement a meagre winter diet. In parts of the country, the moorhen population has been drastically depleted by the release of mink into the wild. The adult birds provide food for foxes and stoats, while the chicks fall prey to herons and pike – mink upset the natural balance and the moorhen, along with many other riverbank dwellers, have simply disappeared. With its distinctive white flash on the underside of its tail, the moorhen (*mere – or pond* hen) is usually found rummaging around in waterside vegetation looking for food.

Early ploughing will bring in the seagulls although it's suspected that many of these birds hardly ever see the sea. The name for the gull comes from the old Welsh *gwylan*, meaning 'wailing bird', because of its mournful cry and in folklore they were believed to be the souls of drowned fishermen and sailors lost at sea. In country weather lore:

*Seagull, seagull, sit on the sand*
*It's never fine weather when you're on the land*

**An extract from *A Treasury of the Countryside*, published in 2003**

In this example we have left the comfort of the farmhouse kitchen and come out into the country – along the muddy lanes, damp woods and hedgerows to concentrate on the wildlife. Our nature study has paid off and we can paint a convincing picture of what we see around us during the grey, bleak month of February. In this article we can also find history, folklore, weather lore and kitchen craft, and although the piece is probably too long for most magazines, it could be cut into two or three shorter pieces, and submitted to different editors.

## Marketplace

**Publications for the 'bred in the bone' type of people, who see the countryside as an integral part of their lives, livelihood and heritage [i.e. *Country Life, The Field, Scottish Field, Irish Countrysports & Country Life, Scottish Sporting Gazette*].**

This is the top end of the genre and the most difficult to break into – the glossy magazines we only see in doctors' or dentists' waiting rooms – and usually some months out of date. *Country Life*, first published in 1897, is the most popular and is primarily concerned with rural communities and their environments as well as the concerns of country dwellers and landowners, field sports, country houses, architecture and gardening, having a diverse readership in the UK and overseas. *The Field*, however, is the world's oldest country and field sports magazine, having been published continuously since 1853, and champions rural pursuits, people and the environment.

*Irish Countrysports & Country Life Magazine* is a field sports and country lifestyle magazine formerly known as *The Irish Hunting, Shooting and Fishing Magazine*. It is published quarterly in association with the Great Game Fairs of Ireland and features seasonal articles on hunting, fishing, shooting, deer stalking, gamekeeping, gundogs, art, antiques, property, interior design and conservation. While *The Scottish Sporting Gazette & International Traveller* is a 'coffee table' annual which concentrates itself on all things Scottish.

As we can see, there is very little opportunity here for the ordinary writer unless we are actively involved in field sports, equestrian or the county/game fairs at a high-flying level. Nevertheless, it is important to be familiar with the style and content of these publications because they merely represent another facet of the fascinating spectrum of country writing. And who knows, we *may* one day find ourselves occupying the slot once held by Ian Niall for so many years.

## Exercise: Market Research

For this exercise we treat ourselves to one of these glossy publications and keep them as a spur to perfecting and developing our own style of country writing. I keep two copies of the now defunct *Country Illustrated* in my in-tray. This, in my opinion, was the best country magazine ever published and I can lay claim to having a five-page extract from *Champagne & Slippers* published in its hallowed pages and one Letter to the Editor! Take them out periodically and study the techniques of the Masters (pun intended!) – see how they refer to wildlife and rural topics – because we *know* we will eventually be able to

27

reach that standard.

**But in the meantime, let's learn a few more writers' tricks of the trade**. Much of the advice on market research advises the freelance writer to study the magazine from cover to cover – including adverts and the letters page to discover the type of readership the editor is aiming to please. This is sound advice and should be thoroughly adhered to at all times and on every occasion – until you know better!

Realistically, market research can be an expensive business if you're going to do it properly. There are hundreds of back issues of magazines available from many different sources – i.e. charity shops, jumble sales, etc., but these can be sadly out of date by the time you settle down to study them. It's a great exercise for the beginner but if you want to break into the 'glossies' or daily newspapers, then your reading needs to be bang up to date.

A recent exercise necessitated the study of monthly glossies to see where a particular feature could be offered. Six magazines were thought to be potentially suitable target markets and as a result there was a charge of £17.20 on the credit card! Expensive this research business – and no guarantee that any of the publications would accept the proposal. Short of huddling behind the magazine racks in my local newsagent trying to read every current publication without drawing attention to myself, there seems no alternative. The glacial stares of disapproval from the shop assistant will cut short the browsing time of even the most hardened hack. Like all hard and fast rules, however, there's usually a short cut, and market research for serious writers is no exception.

The quickest and easiest way to discover whether we can empathise with the readership is to read the regular columnist. Every quality magazine and newspaper has its regulars – they are usually celebrities and are invited to contribute because they identify (in the editor's eye) with the readership. And we can read a column in those precious minutes before the sales assistant realises what we're up to. The columnist will inform us whether the magazine is worth studying further from a submissions point of view.

The regular columnist sets the tone for the magazine and by studying their individual styles a very distinct blueprint will soon evolve for each publication. Extroverted people who have a lot to say about everything and anything to provide a welcome dose of humour, or a spot of controversy, generally write these personal columns. As Brendan Hennessy observed in *Writing Feature Articles*: "Personal columns can bring depth and perspective to the consideration of events. They can provoke thought, move to action, inspire, uplift, to a greater degree than any other kind of article. Star columnists can sell papers – even those dealing in such specialized areas as personal advice, fashion, shopping, sports, recreation and seasonal topics."

As I've already mentioned, one of the most talented and diverse columnists is RWF Poole, the former country diarist from *The Daily Telegraph's* Weekend supplement. The acerbic stance he took over matters country were a sheer delight to his fans but the message he put across was loud and clear – don't interfere with country matters if you don't know what you're talking about. Neither was there room for the fluffy-bunnies approach to county living since this was the territory of the hunting-shooting-fishing brigade. Unfortunately, the incoming editor didn't agree… A similar style might be might be acceptable for *Country Living* or *The Field*, but it would give the editors of *Country Living* and *The Countryman* a fit of the vapours.

# March: The first month of spring

This is the time of year when there is an explosion of activity in the countryside, not just on the farm but in the fields, hedgerows and woodland, as everything awakes from its winter slumber. Of course, as far as the writer is concerned, our 'Spring' piece will have been submitted well before the Christmas holidays, hopefully reflecting current weather conditions and resisting the urge to write about lambs and daffodils! We've received the writer's complimentary copy of the magazine and are now awaiting payment.

So far, we have seen how all sorts of country interests have been introduced to create the scene for a farmhouse kitchen and what we can see in the 'great outdoors'. What we must not overlook is the fact that apart from the inclusion of the Battersbys accident, there is nothing *original* in either article. The secret is in the writer's personal style or technique and the way they draw the reader into their world for a few brief moments. Even the most hardened farmer or seasoned countryman can often be caught taking a moment 'to stand and stare' when some natural happening catches his eye. A fox pouncing on a beetle... an evening flight of starlings... the glorious tones of light and shade of a bluebell wood... a couple of hares at play... a field of corn waving in the breeze... There's a fine line between appreciation and sentiment but the professional writer knows exactly which path to tread when it comes to submitting material for a specific magazine. We may not expect to find country people willing to express their opinions on Nature but there's plenty of material to be had in interviewing them about the jobs they do. And then there are the incomers who bring their work with them – all of interest to editors of country publications.

## Working from Home

Working from home is on the rise among country dwellers and this could be one of the prime considerations when thinking about moving to the country. All that space, freedom and independence... time to potter in the garden, going for long, healthy walks with the dog, dropping in on friends for coffee and a leisurely lunch at the pub.

Needless to say it doesn't quite work like that, simply because it is extremely hard to draw up work/life boundaries when working from home. And it is even more difficult to concentrate when surrounded by personal effects because around the home there's always a job that needs doing. As a result, instead of 'working' we indulge in some displacement activity, like turning out the wardrobe or weeding the rose bed. Added to this, in farming communities there are few people about who have the time for morning coffee, or an extended pub lunch. Because we don't see anyone there is the temptation to slop around in tatty jumpers and leggings – and then we can't answer the door to a caller because we're ashamed of the way we look!

Not so long ago, however, *The Daily Telegraph* published a report on the positive contributions being made by 'incomers' in that many were creating jobs and safe-guarding services by setting themselves up as computer consultants, marketing advisors, accountants and freelance writers: in other words, making a significant contribution to the economy of the community. Many of them may have moved out of town heading for the 'Good Life', but a large number have brought their entrepreneurial skills with them.

And country magazine editors will always be interested in articles on the successes of those who have turned their hands to 'cottage industry' and made it work. Some have opened B&Bs in tourist areas while others have taken over village shops cum Post Offices and, implementing some new ideas, have turned things around for the benefit of the community and inspired others.

Who works from home in your locality? What do they do? The work doesn't necessarily have to be country-related, so long as it reflects business success in the rural heartlands.

"I get up early, take the dog out and then have breakfast before reading the morning paper," says Sue Davenport, who's writing her third novel. "Then it's time to tackle the housework, with each room having a specific day for a good farm out. This takes me up to 'elevenses' and after a cup of coffee I work right through until four o'clock without a break. That gives me enough time to shower, change, get a meal ready and have the evening free. Having said all that, it took me a good two years before I could discipline myself to keep to a tight work schedule. And it wasn't easy," she confided in an interview for *Signposts For Country Living*.

Polly Langford started Just Woodland Friends Introductions over 20 years ago from her rural retreat in Wales, offering a friendly but effective introduction service, matching people who have interests in country living and rural activities. During that time she has given numerous interviews for magazines and newspapers, not to mention the odd radio slot and co-authored *WLTM: The Dating Game*. Because the business is often seasonal or spasmodic, she supplements her income by providing a 'dog-sitting' service for local people who can drop their pets off for the day, over the weekend, or while they are away on holiday or a business trip. She occasionally minds a brace of local donkeys.

Another lady living locally offers a cake decorating service – folk take home-made or shop-bought cakes (large and/or small) to be turned into a themed choice for a party or special occasion. And any competent freelance writer can produce an interview or profile simply because it requires no insider knowledge or experience of the countryside to write about it – all we need is a familiarity with editorial requirements to get our foot in the door and a talent for talking to people. And it could provide us with our first fee-paying submission in our new writing career.

The obvious choice for a March article would be something about the Spring or Vernal Equinox – but how do we find something seasonal but different? I came up with this…

## Life As It Is Lived: Times & Tides

Life in the countryside is governed by seasonal times and tides, and nowhere is this more evident than on the seashore. Since the beginning of time, when man first stood on the shoreline and wondered at the vastness of the ocean, it has been recognised that tides were connected with the moon. Nowhere else on earth was Nature's power and glory so much in evidence.

In *Sea & Seashore*, Sir Isaac Newton's words are used to explain the tides as being due to the moon's gravitational pull on the water, lifting it to form a bulge resembling an enormous wave-crest. There are two such bulges, one on the side of the earth facing the moon, and the other on the earth's far side, for there the moon's pull draws the earth away from the water. Between the two bulges the water is lowered, as though in the trough between these gigantic wave-crests. The friction between the water and the rotating earth slows the movement of these bulges, so that instead of being exactly beneath the moon, they lag a little behind. For this reason, *high tide*, as the bulge is called, does not occur exactly when the moon is overhead, but somewhat later.

"The sun's gravitational pull similarly raises tides akin to, but less powerful than, those caused by the moon – but the two interact. At full and new moon, when the sun and moon are in a straight line with the earth – at intervals of about a fortnight – they co-operate to produce an especially powerful *spring tide*. This has nothing to do with the season: spring tides occur throughout the year and rise higher and fall lower than usual, although the lowest spring tides of the year occur around the Spring Equinox. At the first and third quarters, when the sun and moon form a right angle with the earth – the pull conflicts, making a *neap tide* whose range is unusually small."

But, let us return to the sea… in mid ocean, the tides, like ordinary waves, are simply a rhythmic rise and fall of the water. On the continental shelf, however, they act like the waves on a beach, and become a bodily rush of the water towards, or away, from the land. The rising water produces the tide's flow or flood; its fall is the ebb, and between them, when the tide is almost at a standstill, there are brief periods of slack water. This rise and fall takes place twice every day, but high or low tides occur about 50½ minutes later each day and alter drastically throughout the month. While most shores have two high tides every day, some have only one, and some none at all.

Besides the familiar tides of the **ocean-tides**, there are also two other examples to take into account. **Earth-tides**, the alternating slight change of shape of the Earth due to the gravitational action of the sun and moon, and **atmospheric-tides** of the alternating slight motions of the atmosphere, caused by the moon drawing away the envelope of air that surrounds the Earth to produce regular daily atmospheric tides.

Research has revealed more evidence of the effects of these earth-tides, showing that parts of western Britain and Ireland, for example, 'bounce' by four inches and that the movement is caused as tides ebb and flow twice daily! According to a spokesman for the project, when the tide is in, the extra weight of the water on the continental shelf pushes the adjoining crust down a few inches. At low tide, the Earth springs back. "Because tidal ranges are greater on the south-western side of the British Isles, that is where the biggest bounce can be found." The western tip of England, west Wales, the Western Isles and southern Ireland have the biggest range of movements.

Let us also remind ourselves of the research carried out on oysters transported from their 'home' to a distant location. In laboratory tanks the oysters still displayed a marked tidal rhythm, opening their shells to feed at high tide, and closing at the ebb at their former home. During the first days of their move, the pattern in the tank remained the same; but after two weeks, the oysters were no longer opening and closing in harmony with the tide that washed their distant 'home' but now opened up at the time the tide *would have been locally*... had the town been on a seashore, and not perched on the bank of Lake Michigan, some 580 feet above sea level!

From the week after the Spring or Vernal Equinox we spend a lot of time scanning the skies for a first glimpse of our returning swallows. The observance of the arrival and departure of our migrating swallows are two of the most notable British signposts of the passing of the seasons, wrote Stefan Buczacki in *Fauna Britannica*. "Uniquely graceful, streamlined and masters of the air, swallows occupy a special place in animal folklore and human affection."

Swallows spend most of their time in flight and seldom touch the ground, except for collecting mud to be used for nest building. Each bird returns to the same nesting site every year, despite the fact that they are estimated to fly 1.25 million miles during a lifetime. That is why we always leave their nests intact, ready for when they return.

According to country-lore, if they fly high, fine weather is assured – and there may be more truth in this than mere bird associated weather lore. Insects that feed the swallows are more likely to be carried aloft on thermals when the weather is warm and settled. While Anglo-Saxon farmers believed that if they destroyed a *swallewes* nest then their cows would give bloody milk. We now know that the birds feed upon the flies that spread mastitis – a disease of cattle that tints milk red.

I have two very vivid memories of the arrival and departure of swallows marking the Spring and Autumn Equinoxes. The first is of one spring morning in Wales when I was out walking the dog. We'd just reached the boundary hedge on the upper slope above the farmhouse when a single swallow appeared. It barely had the strength left to clear the hedge but it flew, straight as an arrow, heading for our barn further down the valley. By the time I'd completed the walk and returned to the yard, he was sitting on the wires trying to clean the dirt from his chest feathers. It was one of those magical country moments, being out in the fields at the *precise* moment when our first swallow returned home.

The second occurred when visiting friends in Leicestershire. I stood on top of a small hump in the middle of a cornfield on the day of the Autumn Equinox, completely surrounded by hundreds of whirling swallows, gathering for the flight to Africa. It was another amazing moment to stand there with birds skimming all around my head and feet; and to be at the centre of their chittering as they skimmed through the air like fighter-pilots. The next day they were gone... and the fields were full of silence.

**Submitted for the April 2013 issue of *The Countryman***

As we can see, this article is, yet again, different from the previous two in that it is taking a more scientific view of another aspect of the countryside – or in this case – the seashore. It uses quotes from various academic sources to paint pictures of the way the sun and the moon cause widespread reactions here on earth on a *daily* basis, and which a lot of readers don't know about. But the 'time and tides' tie in with the Spring Equinox, 'spring' tides, and the return of the swallows, rather than more traditional subjects. And not a lamb or daffodil to be seen!

## Marketplace

**Farming publications provide the farming community with the latest developments in fertilizers, foodstuffs, machinery and livestock maintenance [i.e. *Farmers Weekly*, *NFU Countryside Magazine*, the *Farmers Journal* (Ireland), *Farming Magazine***

(USA), *Australian Farm Journal*]. **Some offer a couple of pages of more domestic matters as a concession to the female of the species!**

The rural idyll may have been kindled by a monthly subscription to *Country Living* or a regular supply of Jilly Cooper novels – neither of which feature plunging naked into a slurry channel in mid-winter to rescue an idiot piglet who's just fallen in. *Country Living* and Cooper don't 'do' pig slurry but *real* farmers do. Again this is not an area where fools should rush madly in, because the editor will not look kindly on material from those with no farming background or experience. Some farming magazines do include a section of more domestic articles aimed at the farmer's wife and family, and these might be worth consideration if you can fulfil the editorial requirements.

For the beginner, however, one aspect of farming that we can tackle is anything relating to Farmers' Markets because more and more people want to know where their food comes from, as is shown by the growing popularity of the markets and the spread of more detailed labelling in family butchers. In fact, in the past few years, farmers' markets have become an established feature in old market squares, halls and high streets throughout the country.

The National Association of Farmers' Markets have compiled a directory of all registered farmers' markets across the country and if there's one near you, go along and see what's on offer. One food writer interviewed for *Signposts For Country Living* and who weekends at the family's cottage in Dorset where her husband runs a shoot said: "I wouldn't have a real understanding of food, the thing I work with, if I didn't mix with the farmers. One of my best friends is the dairy farmer and I get all my meat down there, and game."

Local farmers' markets are advertised in most local papers and, although many are still held monthly, more and more are now being held weekly, and the choice of produce is expanding all the time. There are now wide selections of garden plants on sale and these are springing up alongside the stalls selling beef, farmhouse cheese, home-made pickles and organic fruit and vegetables. As one new customer quickly found out, "You'll find people doing their weekly shop there because the food is much fresher than any supermarket can offer."

We need to remember that supposedly 'fresh' supermarket food has often been shipped around the world, either in chilled storage containers, or sealed in inert gas bags to slow down the rotting process. Some 'fresh' food can actually be more than six months old. People are finding that they prefer the taste of fresh food – sprouts from a farmers' market that may have been picked earlier in the morning, for example. As a result, the markets are becoming a normal part of shopping rather than something unusual.

Farming magazines will also be interested in the way other farmers are diversifying to bring in extra income to the farm. There have been some amazing schemes in recent years – including a mock WWI battlefield complete with trenches! Keep your eyes and ears open for anything unusual happening in your area and ask for an interview before someone else does. But don't just confine your writing to the home front (excuse another pun)... check the following out online for other ideas because overseas organizations might also be interested in what's going on in other countries.

FARMA: National Farmers Retail & Markets Association UK www.farma.org.uk

National Directory for Farmers Markets (USA) www.farmers market.com/

Australian Farmers' Markets Association www.farmers markets.org.au/

## Exercise: Developing an Idea

Producing good, marketable ideas in freelance writing is just the same as preparing a vegetable garden and needs the same formula of sowing, fertilising, watering, pruning and, following the harvesting, new and exciting ways of serving and/or preserving. Once an idea begins to germinate, resist the urge to get it down on paper and into the post box. Many a good idea has fallen on stony ground by an overzealous application of enthusiasm. It doesn't matter how the idea is eventually going to manifest, the development stages are going to be the same. We make as many notes as possible and let the idea run around in our mind; play with the idea, tease it but we don't make any attempt to write down the first thing that comes into our head.

What we are looking for is the original slant that is going to 'hook' the editor's attention and hold it, right through to the very last line. Don't forget that most editors have seen it all before, so they will be looking for a different treatment to delight their readership. It's not always as easy as it sounds to come up with something original and exciting and, as we all know, there's nothing new under the sun – or in creative writing.

**Sowing** the idea is the easy part but before doing anything else with our notes, try looking at the article from a different angle or perspective. If the original idea was intended for the incoming couple, then try looking at it through the eyes of a farmer's wife, rural businessman or elderly country person. Each pair of eyes will see the situation from a different angle – and this applies to all forms of writing.

A good **fertilising** agent is the perusal of magazines, books and newspapers where we think the finished piece might appear. The house style of the publication will indicate the approach and language acceptable by the editor and put us in the position of communicating directly with the readership via the advertisements and content. In other words: researching our intended market so we know exactly who we're writing for. If our idea is for a full-length book then our fertilising techniques need to be even more far reaching. Here we need to take into account what's already in publication and what's about to be published, especially when it comes to non-fiction country books. Publishers don't want a repeat of what someone else is doing (or has done) so the wider our knowledge of the marketplace, the better chance you have of producing something original for our proposal.

**Watering** our idea with plenty of carefully researched material gives an impression of space and depth even with the most economical use of words. Our articles need to contain original material that hasn't appeared in print before (usually the 'idea' behind writing the thing in the first place). This is one of the most important stages, since over-writing can drench the piece with superfluous description, while under-writing usually leaves the reader struggling to empathise, sympathise or disagree.

**Pruning (or editing)** our work is something else that shouldn't be rushed – but when in doubt, dig it out. By now your idea will have grown into something quite large and impressive but it's got to be tailor-made for your target market, so start looking for ways to make it slicker and sharper. Don't be tempted to send some long rambling saga when the maximum length for submission is 1200 words. It may be that you've too much information for a full-length non-fiction book, so look at those odd paragraphs that don't really fit, even if they do contain interesting anecdotes. Take them out and use them for articles to promote the book's theme in other magazines (especially if you're writing on a specialist subject). If the articles sell, enclose copies with the proposal when it goes off to a publisher. This shows an interest on the marketing front. Whatever we write about, there is *always* too much detail in the first draft and the mark of the professional is knowing when and what to cut.

**Harvesting** ensures we have several possible market outlets in mind. This doesn't mean that we're going to send the *identical* piece to each of them – are you? Each publication has an independent house style and so our submission needs to be compatible. We've come back to understanding what editors want, and we can never have too much information in this department. We make it our business to find out what's going on in this area of the publishing world because just as much attention needs to be paid to marketing our work as writing it.

And finally, when **serving up** our finished piece, don't spoil all this hard work and effort by submitting a poorly presented manuscript – or in the wrong format. More and more editors are accepting online proposals/submissions but check in advance if this is the way they do business. If not, send by post, but don't forget the stamped-addressed envelope if you want a reply.

### Preserving an Idea

What happens if your wonderful idea isn't quite ready for working on? Notes... notes... and more notes. Keep a notebook by you at all times and jot down anything and everything that comes into your mind. We often find that whenever we've had an idea, we'll find information comes our way without looking for it; often in the form of related subjects appearing in the media. Keep notes from the TV and radio, and cuttings from magazines and newspapers. We won't use everything, but a line here or a quote there will help to add depth and credibility to our writing – especially when we're just starting out. The professional writer learns to recognise these 'extras' and not rely on using the same old themes over and over again.

Some writers believe that too much market information stifles creativity but it pays to know your markets as most successful writers will tell you. A good idea is all very well, but if we haven't learned how to nurture and develop it, then it may shrivel and die. Ideas are the lifeblood of creative writing and, when all is said and done, this piece started off as a throw-away comment about the similarities between writing and growing vegetable marrows!

Explore the Farmers' Markets and diversification operations

in your area and pick a particular subject that could provide an article or interview suitable for a farmers' publication, or regional magazine. Try to find a perspective or topic that is a little bit out of the ordinary and then put your own brand of 'spin' to make it marketable. Even a B&B can be made to sound interesting if there have been any famous guests staying there, such as HRH the Prince of Wales!

# April: Rain and sunshine both together

We're sitting in the bar at The Fox (our local hostelry) when George, the barman, points out that the group of ladies in the corner is the local writers' group, who meet there once a month. He of the perfect proportions opens his mouth to make some recommendation on my behalf, when his 'brilliant idea' is strangled at birth by the steely glint in my eye.

"What's the matter?" he asks, as George moves away to attend to the leader of the group who looks as though she could arm-wrestle a Shire stallion and not be on the losing side.

"One whiff of the fact that I'm a full-time writer and there'll be more manuscripts unearthed in this neck of the woods than are dreamt of in your philosophy," I hiss. "The follow-up line for anyone introduced as a writer is: Will you have a quick look at my novel?" He looks doubtful, but says nothing more on the subject. The evening passes off pleasantly, the ladies get quietly merry, and we leave without anyone being any the wiser about my method of earning a living.

A week later, however, my cover has been blown. "I wonder if you'd have a look at my manuscript!?" a strident voice demands across a crowded room. I glare but Mr Wonderful refuses to meet my eye; he's fighting a losing battle with an uncontrollable grin. The voice belongs to the Shire wrestler and I later discover that her husband owns some of the finest shooting land in the County. This is a world inaccessible to 'incomers' but I've been invited to the 'Big House' for coffee – the local postmistress is impressed, or so the postman informed me.

I appreciate this is how things are done in the country but I really don't have the time or inclination to make polite noises about someone's work just to keep the social merry-go-round well oiled. I earn my living as a writer and I'm not in the market for freebie consultations for the simple reason that there's no such thing as a 'quick look', you either read the damned thing properly and give a fair assessment, or you refuse point blank – and then no one talks to you at the point-to-point.

Oh well, I suppose I'll get used to bending the new rules but it never ceases to amaze me that despite the fact that our nearest neighbour is a mile away, everyone already has an intimate knowledge of our home life

**Published in the April 2000 issue of** *The New Writer*

## A Cautionary Tale

And the moral of *that* story is never let on that you're a writer because you'll be reeled in to help with all sorts of local 'writing' jobs – even writing, compiling, editing and publishing the parish magazine! All of it time-consuming – and none of it fee paying. It may be gratifying to be included in community events but do think twice before you volunteer, because it can be extremely tricky to extract yourself. No one else wants the job and that was why you were offered it in the first place – in much the same way as being invited on to the parish council!

This area is a minefield for writers and we will return to the subject later in the year; but for the time being, let's stick to what we know and not rush into something we don't fully understand...

## Life As It Is Lived: Or If It's Got Fur or Feathers It Bites!

Before deciding to go tramping about the highways and byways, it is a good time to reflect on what we *personally* mean by 'the countryside'. For a healthy natural balance it is necessary for British farming to be more than just the maintenance of a landscape that people like to look at and walk in. It is an accepted fact that two-thirds of agricultural land is pasture – i.e. grassland. Left to its own devices, land will quickly regress to scrub and, ultimately, reforestation. If grass is not maintained on a large scale by the grazing of animals, it will not remain grass for very long, and once farmland ceases to be farmed, it will soon become a tangle of brambles and other intrusive cover. The only way in which the necessary grazing can be provided is by livestock farming and only large grazing animals can fulfil this need.

Many would like to see livestock farming disappear from the landscape. "We had a family of New-Agers move into the village, and it wasn't long before they started telling us how wrong livestock farming was," said one local farmer. "According to them, all the animals should be allowed to roam free, since there was no need to kill them for food. They couldn't grasp that if livestock weren't in the fields to be reared for meat, then there wouldn't be any sheep or cattle *anywhere* in the landscape; and no fields either. This sort of cloud cuckoo land philosophy is best kept in the towns where it belongs, and won't win anybody any friends round here."

The countryside is where people live and make a living, either through agriculture or livestock, and while there will always be bad farmers, they *are* in the minority. Those who have been farming the land for generations do not need advice on animal rights, welfare or liberation, and it only fuels ill-feeling if those expressing such opinions do so without any personal, first-hand knowledge, or experience of farm management.

It's also a good idea to keep in mind that in the countryside, even the mildest mannered of creatures will react if it's not handled or approached correctly. In the lifestyle magazines psychologists are always explaining how to read the body language of our friends and colleagues – well, country people do the same with their livestock. Because they know when an animal is likely to be aggressive or a touch menopausal, they steer clear of the field or paddock until the danger is past.

It also pays to remember that despite the campaign to publicise the countryside as a ramblers' paradise, domestic animals don't read the small print. If we want to walk across an open field when the bull has been turned out with the heifers, then be ready to break into a sprint should he decide to lower his head and charge. Sheep and pigs with young can also be pretty aggressive – and even a shortcut through the farmyard could offend the sensibilities of a territorial cockerel or sheepdog. If we do decide to wander off the designated footpaths and on to private land, then we must be prepared for the consequences.

**Sheep:** There was the well-publicised incident that caused a great deal of mirth some years ago when a contestant at the Leeds International Piano Festival was assaulted by a sheep during his relaxation period. The commentators felt it was highly hilarious and incongruous that a sheep should be the perpetrator of such an indignity, but sheep have their moments too, especially during the lambing season.

**Cattle:** When a farmer went to investigate why a group of his bullocks were huddled in the corner of the field, he found a middle-aged lady and her dog perched precariously in the lower branches of a tree. Cattle are inquisitive creatures and a whole herd breaking into a run can be an alarming sight. Another dog walker had to undergo four hours of surgery after being trampled by a herd of 35 cows.

**Horses:** As herd animals, horses will instinctively react to the rest breaking into a wild gallop across the field, especially if there is a dog loose. Most horses are good natured, but those that have the urge to bite can inflict a nasty wound given half a chance.

**Pigs:** An enraged sow protecting her young will attack a human and is capable of inflicting fatal injuries. Don't be fooled by the public image of the Tamworth Two!

**Goats:** Even those that have been de-horned can knock a fully-grown man off his feet. They are immensely strong and incredibly stubborn, which does not always bode well for the naïve would-be goat keeper. Ours escaped and kept the vicar holed up in the telephone box for two hours!

**Chickens:** Cockerels can be some of the most vicious creatures encountered in the farmyard. They are possessed of innate cunning and strike fear into the hearts of service callers such as postmen and meter readers.

Another example of animals not behaving according to human expectations was recorded in *The Countryman's Weekly*, explaining why a docile pet ferret can turn into a wild animal once it starts working. Simply because below ground there are not only rabbits, but also rats, stoats, weasels or even foxes, instinct kicks in and immediately the animal is on the defensive. "When it resurfaces it may be excited, angry or even wounded – and this is where body language comes in; you go to pick the ferret up without understanding this and it turns to bite. Remember that the ferret has just been on another planet. It thinks it is being attacked and defends itself."

Even a pet rabbit can cut up rough and those powerful back legs with their long claws can inflict a nasty wound, as one pet owner recalls: "We bought a rabbit for the kids, but he turned out to be so vicious that no one could get near him. He took to living wild in the garden, and on several occasions I had to go and apologise to neighbours because the damn thing had savaged their cat or dog. It must have been one very lucky bunny, because he actually died of old age. I don't think there was a fox in the neighbourhood who would tackle him!"

**An extract from *Signposts For Country Living*, published in 2010**

In this extract we have moved into another realm of the countryside that covers encounters with *domestic* animals, which often come as an unexpected shock to people new to the exposure to farmland and its occupants. Although it's a light-hearted approach, it nevertheless makes it quite clear that livestock can be extremely dangerous and, with the best will in the world, cannot always be contained, or deemed to be friendly.

## Marketplace

**The 'glossy monthly' that features people, conservation, wildlife, cookery, rural houses and gardens, and country businesses – but rarely found in a working farmhouse kitchen [i.e.** *Country Living, LandLove, Irish Country Magazine, Country Living* **(USA),** *Rural Living Canada***].**

These are the up-market 'glossies' that cater for middle-class people who aspire to living in the country and so there is often an element of glamour or romance, rather than sheer practicality about them. Nevertheless, this type of magazine probably has one of the largest readerships of all the country publications and it is worth our while submitting material – even if initially it's only something for the Letters page, which are often 'paid' in luxury prizes for the 'Letter of the Month'. There's plenty of scope for articles and interviews but it is a very difficult market to break into, so don't be disappointed if it takes time.

And don't be afraid to explore the overseas markets but do make sure you've obtained samples of the magazine before attempting to write for it. The livestock content doesn't cover farming on a grand scale – but the interior articles usually do! We're talking about a moneyed lifestyle and the editor will want material that reflects the aspirations of the readership. Rare breeds go down well here, as does the 'working from home' angle, especially successful rural businesses that could appeal to both UK and overseas publications – so double the fee as you sell FBSR (first British serial rights) and first USA, Canadian or Australian serial rights for overseas.

## Exercise: Selling an Idea

In the March section, we discussed developing an idea so the typescript that finally lands on an editor's desk has a degree of originality in its approach. But first we need to pay attention to selling our idea and this means making sure that the submission letter also has something in it to catch an editor's eye. We've done our market research; we've studied back issues of the magazine so the next step is to send a carefully constructed proposal for two or even three separate articles that should be designed to appeal to the editor. Give a two or three sentence description for each idea, which should convey the feel of the finished article.

The longer the period of research, the more familiar you will be with the type of material the editor likes and, even more important, the subjects which have already been covered in recent back issues. Quite a lot of submissions are rejected purely and simply because the subject matter is too similar to material recently published, or already accepted and/or commissioned. Your proposal letter should state clearly and succinctly what connection you have with the subject and why you are qualified to write the pieces on offer. Give an indication of the length of each piece so the editor knows what to expect and whether it's in accordance with their own guidelines.

Don't complete the piece until the editor e-mails or phones to say they would like to see the finished article. Since every magazine's requirements are different, it would need revamping, unless it had been written with that particular publication in mind. And remember, the acceptance of an idea in principle isn't a commission. The idea might be fantastic but if the finished article doesn't come up to scratch then it will be rejected.

Never submit a complete article with the words: "This article is highly suitable for your publication". Experience shows that someone who's never seen the magazine, and who has probably pulled our name out of one of the writers' handbooks without bothering to send for a copy, has written this sort of letter. The approach is usually incompatible with the guidelines even though there aren't any hard and fast rules about house style. Usually the letter or e-mail refers to me by my first name, and I'm frantically playing mental scrabble, trying to work out who the hell's sent it. And am I supposed to know them? Have I asked for this submission?

Keep things businesslike until you've established regular contact and then be guided by the response you receive. Remember, first impressions *do* count – they can tell an editor whether s/he *wants* to work with you. And this is especially true when it comes to publishers and editors who might be looking at *you* as a long-term project. You only have one chance to make an impression.

As an exercise, we're going to submit a proposal letter to the magazine of your choice, and if you've done your homework properly, you will be aware of:

- what the editor likes;
- and dislikes;
- what's been run before;
- whether a different approach could make interesting reading;
- questions that are regularly asked;
- answers that don't satisfy;
- a need for good fillers;
- new books under discussion;
- old favourite subjects;
- interesting subjects for the Letters page.

Going over your back issues of the magazines there must have been something that triggers off a response; something you thought you'd write a letter about at the time, but never did; or a different slant to a popular theme; an interview with a local rural person.

# May: A foretaste of summer

Country people cope quite happily with eccentricity, but they are not so tolerant of affectation, or indeed being patronised. Neither do they take kindly to complaints about activities that have been going on for centuries. Another contributor to *Signposts For Country Living* recalled a supper party during a visit to some old friends who'd just moved to the country. Her husband began by airing his views on fox hunting and the whole table went quiet. His wife aimed a kick at him under the table so he headed off down the equally emotive path of farming subsidies and it went even quieter. A fourth Ice Age was descending by the time he enthused over the low cost of housing in the area. Embarrassed beyond belief by her spouse's demonstration of complete social ineptitude, she tipped a bowl of liqueured cherries over the immaculate white linen tablecloth. "Needless to say, we haven't been invited back... or anywhere else for that matter. Whenever we go down for a visit, we're kept well away from their new chums."

## Both Sides of the Fence

Visitors to the country often echo 'green' sentiments that British farmers should not be looking to make a profit from farming. They should, it appears, be focusing on the one thing that now matters in the countryside – the environment. As James Douglas remarked acidly in *Country Illustrated*: "This writer has obviously been under the naïve and ignorant misapprehension that, in the course of doing their work and running their businesses, farmers did not make a bad job of looking after the environment." He went on to reflect that generations of farming families had obviously laboured under the misguided belief that when it came to providing the nation with a rural landscape, they hadn't done too bad a job.

Unfortunately, all too often the urban reader is misinformed by publications that offer "seductive solutions to complex issues and rely on a carefully cultivated imagery to avert any awkward questions." There appears to be little thought given to the men who actually put their money, blood, sweat and tears into the land and, hopefully, make a profit from their labours – and pass it on so that succeeding sons and daughters can do the same, always with the hope of making enough money to support future generations. "For a storekeeper to open a shop with the avowed intention of doing anything other than making a profit would seem absurd. Why should farmers be any different?" asked Douglas.

Another countryman objected to regular 'tours' offered by incomers when entertaining visiting friends. Sitting outside a local pub with some friends after watching an afternoon of village cricket, they were treated to a loud voice braying, "What on earth have they done to your village, Brigit? There are cars everywhere. You really must complain to the council."

Many conservation groups would have the public believe that they are the only ones capable of preserving and 'governing' the landscape for posterity, but in reality it's the farmer who is the true custodian of the countryside, and who really understands Nature. The country writer needs to be able to reflect the opinions of *both* sides of the fence if the target market is publication in the rural magazines.

## Life As It Is Lived: Or If It's Got Fur or Feathers – It Bites! (again)

Or at least something that lives *on* it does, as a neighbour found out to his cost when he and his wife 'rescued' a small fox cub from the roadside verge. They phoned the local RSPCA, who told them to put it back where they found it. The cub was duly returned, together with a blanket, a hot water bottle and a large plate of dog food! When they returned an hour later the cub's mother had obviously retrieved it and all was well until the couple got home and found that their bodies were a mass of red flea bites, and the dogs were scratching themselves silly. Baby Reynard had left them a rather unwelcome 'thank you' present.

Hedgehogs also carry an impressive amount of personal livestock, despite the Mrs Tiggywinkle persona, so beware of picking one up. Hedgehog fleas are different from cat and dog fleas, but fleas from one species can transfer to another on a temporary basis, as many dogs and humans will testify, although members of the medical profession may tell us otherwise!

Bats often find themselves grounded in daylight hours, having been attacked by a cat. Again, these tiny creatures will bite when frightened and, as they can carry rabies, are best left to specialists to handle. Remember that bats are a protected species and even if they invade your home you are not allowed to remove or disturb them. If it does become necessary to move one for its own safety, make sure you're wearing a stout pair of gardening gloves.

Recently a rural community found itself subjected to regular buzzard attacks because the footpath to a new housing development took pedestrians and cyclists too close to where the birds were nesting. There were lots of protests but again the buzzard is a protected species; and in any case, it was only protecting its young from what it viewed as intruders in its territory.

Wild animals have no concept of being 'rescued' as one hunt saboteur discovered and was most indignant because the fox he'd pounced on to 'save', turned around and bit him quite badly in the face. To the fox *his* behaviour was seen as threatening and the animal reacted accordingly. Wild animals do not stop to rationalise whether we mean them harm or not and are best left to their own devices, unless their situation is life-threatening.

## What you can and can't do:

**Rabbits:** As long as you do not set out to cause deliberate suffering you do not need permission to kill rabbits and there is no limit to the number you can kill. In fact, under regulations dating from 1952 you are obliged to control rabbits on your land, although this does not mean completely eradicating them.

**Mink:** Mink farming was banned on the supposition that it is cruel to farm animals for their skin alone and those in the wild today are the descendants of escapees, or those misguidedly released by animal activists. As the result of new legislation, mink is to be eradicated from Britain and landowners are encouraged to kill or trap them; it is illegal to release them once caught. Trapping mink, however, is a hazardous business because a) the animals are extremely vicious; and b) they tend to share their environment with highly protected otters and polecats.

**Moles:** Despite its cute *Wind in the Willows* reputation, no other animal causes as much devastation to gardens and pastureland as the mole. You rarely get to see one, but you will certainly notice the mess they leave behind. Farmers who make a lot of silage cannot risk soil contamination of the cut grass (which can cause listeriosis in sheep), and so they are keen to keep mole populations to a minimum on their land. Spring traps are designed to kill moles and are exempt from legislation, with no permission required to use them.

**Badgers:** No longer rare, but it is illegal to disturb their setts in any way under pain of a £5,000 fine or six months in jail for every animal killed unless approved by DEFRA. Badger setts are recognisable by the evidence of paw prints, hair, grass and hay outside – but no droppings, which they bury in pits.

**Grey squirrels:** Still regarded as an alien species that must be killed if caught as they are responsible for the decimation of the native red squirrel population, and for killing young trees and saplings. If you unintentionally catch one in a trap you will be breaking the law if you let it go!

The so-called 'Section Six' animals that cannot be harmed or disturbed without permission from DEFRA are bats, wildcats, dormice, hedgehogs, pine martens, common otters, polecat shrews and the red squirrel. If any of these animals were accidentally caught in a trap you would be breaking the law if you did not return them at once to the wild.

**An extract from** *Signposts For Country Living,* **published 2010**

Many readers and writers of 'country matters' prefer to steer clear of the realities of dealing with wildlife when it comes up close and personal. For most newcomers the first livestock they acquire usually manifests itself in the form of half a dozen hens – which quickly become family pets, all with names and identities. The family takes a great deal of pleasure from the hens milling around and producing fresh eggs for breakfast. Then the unthinkable happens. Our youngest goes up to collect the eggs and discovers the mangled bodies and feathers all over the place – and not a hen in sight. Suffice to say, a fox's rampage in the hen house has altered quite a lot of perceptions about this controversial creature.

If foxes become a problem, trapping and snaring are allowed, but far more landowners these days prefer to control numbers by 'lamping.' This involves going out at night with a rifle and a very bright light. A fox, being naturally curious, will stand and stare at the approaching lamp, giving a marksman a chance to shoot it. Shooting is, of course, often the urban dweller's only concession to culling, but as countryman RWF Poole has observed many times in the past, "There is a shadowy figure who in anti-hunting folklore is the definitive answer for both fox and deer control – the 'skilled marksman with a high-powered rifle'. While such people do exist, a lot of people with high-powered rifles are far from skilled and, as a result, shooting accounts for more animal suffering than most country people feel is necessary."

Urban foxes have taken the debate into the towns in recent

years with a growing number of reported cases of attacks on domestic pets and babies – one even had the temerity to bite a lawyer's ear off as she was sleeping safe and sound in her own bed! Farmers' claims that rural foxes will take lambs and piglets have been scornfully dismissed by the powers-that-be as a 'rural myth' but the mounting evidence is not favourable for 'Charlie' and his chums. So, make sure you listen to both sides of the argument.

## Marketplace

**Some magazines maintain a rather genteel and romantic/nostalgic approach to country matters, that doesn't really reflect a true picture as they resolutely refuse to feature any reference to livestock farming (unless to 'rare breeds'), field sporting events or culling, which are still very much an integral part of rural life [i.e. *The Countryman, This England, Evergreen, Country Magazine* (USA), *Australian Country Crafts*].**

Like most country writers, I have a soft spot for what is possibly one of the most popular of the rural publications – *The Countryman* magazine – founded in 1927 and edited by Paul Jackson for many years. The editor does, however, involve himself in environmental and conservation issues, and has observed: "In publishing you quickly learn there's more than one side to every story..." which means he *will* give space to Robin Page, both sides of the 'ragwort debate', vermin control, the pros and cons of 'endangered species' or population growth. This is a monthly publication, with a content so diverse the only way to know what to submit is by taking out a subscription.

*This England*, founded in 1968, has a strong overseas following and describes itself as a "celebration of England and all things English; famous people, natural beauty, towns and villages, history, traditions, customs and legends, crafts, etc., but nothing controversial. Generally, a rural basis, with the 'Forgetmenots' section publishing readers' recollections and nostalgia." Published quarterly, they receive a high number of submissions each week, so study the back issues on the website and make sure you don't duplicate material already covered. *Evergreen* magazine comes from the same stable.

Again, it's worth looking at overseas publications as these may be interested in some 'Old Country' nostalgia – providing it's not overly sentimental and has a practical approach. Most magazines have a website and this should give a good indication of what's been published in the past year and the type of material the editor is looking for. The best submissions will be those that form some link between the two countries, with which the reader can identify.

**We must also be conscious of what *not* to write about for each individual magazine.**

Make a study of the 'causes' championed by the editor in each issue as the various organisations are given space in the form of advertisements and editorials. There are all sorts of conservation groups, wildlife trusts and rural campaigns that will tell us who the campaigners hope to be reaching to drum up support. A lot of money has been spent on finding out this kind of information and it is another writer's shortcut to market research. If the editor appears to be astutely avoiding your 'cause' then don't offer to write about it.

## Exercise: The Hook

How many times do we read (or heed) the advice about hooking an editor's attention? How many writers fail to appreciate the fact that if the editor (or publisher, or agent) isn't hooked right from the start our submission *will* be rejected? And it doesn't matter whether we are talking about non-fiction or fiction, short stories or novels, poetry or prose – it must have that sharp barb to make the reader want to turn the page. If it fails to entice in the opening sentences, then we will be lucky if the professional reader even bothers to go on to the next paragraph.

## But what exactly is a hook?

It is a simple device for introducing our subject matter or story with impact, rather than long-winded preamble. That opening line or first paragraph is the most important part of the whole piece. It may be a challenging statement. A question. Brilliant use of language or analogy. Evocative description of a person, place or thing. Except that it really doesn't matter how brilliant the rest of our work may be – an editor isn't even going to bother to read it unless we've hooked their attention right from the start.

Study the magazines of your choice and see how the writers have used the various different openings to introduce an article or topic. Which is the most common form of introduction? Does each one have impact? Is there an element of surprise at the start? Does it use a bold statement? Now make sure that your next submission starts with a bang, not a whimper.

# June: Three fine days and a thunderstorm

Although rural writing focuses on the harsh realities of country living, there is still plenty of scope for nostalgia if it's angled right. People *do* like to share their memories, while others like to read about them and the 'hook' is to stir similar recollections in the hearts and minds of the readers. Childhood retrospection always conjures up blue skies, endless sunny days, buttercup filled meadows and rainbows after a summer storm, but in reality our days weren't filled with picnics, egg and cress sandwiches, Tizer and ginger beer *a la* Enid Blyton's Famous Five stories.

## Finding the Happy Medium

And yet there *were* 'Famous Five moments' and we *can* write about them, if we find a link between the then and now. In *Life-Writes: Where do writers get their ideas from?* I recalled the occasion at the Welsh Game Fair when one of the attractions in the main arena was a chap who was simulating all the old poacher's tricks for the entertainment of the crowd. His display was cleverly contrived by using a series of elastic lures to make the fake 'rabbits' streak across the field into the longnet.

I'd been watching the display with a view to including it in an article about the Fair but instead of taking in the details of the here and now, my subconscious mind was re-living my own memories of poaching that had been long forgotten and it was the running of the longnet that triggered the memory. A longnet was some two foot high and some 20 feet long, and held upright by cut hazel sticks... how did I know they were hazel sticks? Because it had been my job to carry them!

The story goes back to my *pre*-school years and my father left babysitting. Being a countryman, after the war he'd turned his hand to a spot of DIY recreational therapy (i.e. poaching) because that was the way you coped in those pre-counselling days. It was a fine night with a poacher's moon; myself (aged about four) and the dog (about the same age) were bundled on to the motorbike and off we went into the darkness of the woods for a few hours of illegal rabbiting. This happened several times until my mother found out – then there was all hell to pay and my night-time excursions were stopped, but I still enjoy the magic of being alone in remote places during the hours of darkness.

I've included this tale because I've told it (and similar) so many times at writers' workshops as an illustration of how the most unexpected things can trigger a useful memory. It gives the extra personal touch to what may otherwise be a straightforward report of a country fair; it bridges then and now with the added bonus of human interest. **If we write about the past in terms of pure nostalgia, the market is limited; if we use this 'bridging technique' it gives an added dimension as the following example shows:**

## Life As It Is Lived: Bringing In The Hay

At the Summer Solstice, around the time of the full moon, there is no real darkness in the countryside, although the stars in the Plough still gleam valiantly against the deepening night sky. Soft breezes are heavy with the scent of freshly turned hay and late into the night there is the hum of tractors bringing home the last wagon stacked with bales. The race to have the hay stacked in the barn before the rains arrive has been won this year.

The men have been out in the fields since dawn and will be looking forward to the supper spread out on the kitchen table. Although it's school tomorrow, we have been allowed to stay up late to take part in the feast. No standing on ceremony here. The scrubbed boards provide the only backdrop for the huge ham waiting for carving, with its thick outer layer of white fat and breadcrumbs. It's our father's last job for the day and everyone is quickly served with a generous helping of succulent, home-cooked ham. Bowls of crisp salad and juicy tomatoes straight from the garden, and buttered new potatoes lifted just that morning, sprinkled with parsley. Hard-boiled eggs from the hen house and home-made pickles; fresh bread with rich butter and cheese complete the meal.

The men are too tired for conversation and the only sound around the table is the click of knives against plates, accompanied by monosyllabic grunts. They've drunk their fill of cold tea swigged from the bottle during the long days of haymaking, and so endless cups of strong, hot tea are the order of the night. The hour is late but everyone is still in shirtsleeves because the night is hot and sultry, with a threat of a thunderstorm in the air. We fidget from the hayseeds and dried grass that have crept under our clothes and into our shoes, but we don't want to move and break the spell. Unlike the harvest supper that will take place in the village hall in a few months' time, this is a solemn occasion. And yet we are instinctively aware of being involved in some unspoken seasonal mystery that binds our parents to the land.

For our agricultural ancestors, there were only two seasons: summer and winter. Summer was welcomed in with merriment and pageantry as part of its May Day rituals, while the Solstice on 21st June marked the turning point of the year, as the sun began its slow descent into winter. Those far-off midsummer ceremonies involved the lighting of bonfires on hilltops and village greens, around which the local populace would gather. Cattle were driven through the flames to cure any sick animals, and to guard against harm of any kind in the coming year. Young men and girls would jump over the flames to ensure a good harvest and the parents of the young people who bounded the highest over the fire would have the most abundant crop.

The sun was ritually strengthened by bonfires burning everywhere on Midsummer's Eve; with torchlight processions through the streets of the towns, and straw-bound wheels set alight and rolled down steep rural hillsides into the valleys below. By the Middle Ages this was said to be in homage to St John but these midsummer celebrations were considerably older, dating back to pre-Christian times. The bonfires also drove out evil (ill luck) and brought the promise of fertility and prosperity to men, crops and livestock. Lit on the windward side of the fields, the life-giving smoke blew over the crops, while blazing gorse was carried around penned animals to protect them from disease or accident.

Another much later fire custom involved the belief in a magical coal that should be taken 'live' from the hearth on Midsummer's Day between 10 am and 12 noon, and buried in the garden without the person concerned speaking to anyone, to bring luck to the household in the coming year. The luck could also be transferred to anyone finding a piece of buried coal on Midsummer's Day, although the power of the charm varied, as did the plant under which it could be found. A coal discovered under the root of mugwort, for example, would keep the finder safe from plague, carbuncle, lightning, quartan ague and from burning. A piece found under the root of plantain should be placed under the pillow that night, in order to discover the identity of a future husband in a dream.

It's now more than fifty years since those summers of childhood memory, and technology has taken much of the hard labour out of haymaking. That landscape has changed beyond recognition, with most of the Home Counties farmland we freely roamed disappearing under ring roads and urban development. Neighbours no longer gather together for a well-earned supper after labour shared. But all is not lost...

The scene changes, and down in the Glen there is still the drone of a tractor as the scent of new-mown hay wafts gently in on the evening breeze. Cattle stand motionless in the shadows by the hedge. In the gathering dusk we sit round the slate table to share a Midsummer supper with local farming friends now that the day's work is done. The fare isn't so very different, although the enormous ham has given way to a home-baked bacon and egg pie, served with jacket potatoes, and accompanied by a dry white wine or cold beer.

Ash logs burn in the patio brazier to ward off a slight chill in the mountain air and, on the rim of the hill behind the cottage, one by one the stars of the Plough burst into brilliance. We are some days away from the new moon and so the Summer Triangle of Vega, Altair and bright Deneb will be clearly visible later this evening. It's a humbling thought that we are seeing this last star, not as it is now, but as it used to be in the days when these islands were part of the Roman Empire.

Conversation recalls the endless stories of more recent times, all mingled with the history of the Glen. Memories are only a step away in time and the mystery still remains from those far-off summer nights.

**Published in the July 2010 issue of *The Countryman***

As we can see from this article, the bridging-technique spans 50 years to create an almost continuous story – with a little bit of kitchen-lore and astronomy thrown in for good measure! The opening and closing links refer to the stars that were and are visible in the night sky around the Summer Solstice. Everyone pitched in to help the local farmers during haymaking and harvest, and although I have hundreds of memories covering these activities, I took a slightly different slant to attract the editor's attention and set the scene around the supper table after the last of the hay had been brought in.

## Marketplace

**Smallholding publications give practical advice on small-scale poultry and livestock keeping (including rare breeds), country crafts, gardening and cookery. The approach is aimed at those who wish to establish a living from what they produce or rear on the land [i.e. *Country Smallholding, Practical Poultry,***

*Smallholder, Small Farm Canada, Hobby Farm Magazine* USA, *Homesteading* (USA), *Countryside Magazine* (Australia)].

Smallholding, homesteading, hobby farming, small farm are all terms for a piece of land with an adjoining property, including farm buildings, on a much smaller scale than a farm. Usually anything between 3–50 acres and used for small-scale livestock keeping and/or growing vegetables. The definition in Wikipedia states:

> A smallholding offers its owner a means of achieving self-sufficiency as to his and his family's own needs which he may be able to supplement by selling surplus produce at a farmers market and/or temporary booths, or more permanent shop facilities are often part of a smallholding.

There are websites for the USA, Ireland, Canada, Australia and New Zealand, where any of these terms can apply to anyone who 'follows the back-to-the-land movement by adopting a sustainable, self-sufficient lifestyle' without it being a primary source of income. Make enquiries in your locality and find out if anyone has introduced a successful scheme for money-making from farm shops, pick-your-own, fruit juices, etc., that would provide an interesting article. Check out the websites and see if there are online newsletters where the beginner writer can earn their first writing credits. For example:

**www.smallholding.ie**
**www.smallholder.co.uk**
**www.rural-smallholdings.co.uk**
**www.hobbyfarmersassociation.org**

## Exercise: How-To Material

If writing for online sites, newsletters or blogs, your submission needs to be kept short, sharp and concise – and probably not more than 500 words. This type of submission might be better suited to a 'how-to' piece. For this exercise we need to produce something suitable for an online publication that relates to production from a smallholding – poultry keeping, rabbit rearing, vegetable growing, etc. This example was accepted by the online how-to site Howopia, with the information coming from a friend who started this small business from her gardening interests:

### How To Market Home Delivery Vegetable Boxes

The idea of selling boxes of 'delivered to the door' fresh vegetables has been around for a long time but if you have access to lots of home-grown produce, it could an idea for a small business. Look at what you grow yourself and then look at what the growers on local allotments and market gardens are producing: could this be a family business, or a co-operative. Vegetable box schemes seem to be just as successful in towns, village and rural areas where signing up for a weekly delivery of seasonal produce is something that is looked forward to. Consider the following:

### What you'll need:

Plentiful and reliable suppliers
Attractive boxes
Literature for handouts
Tips sheets and recipes
A computer
Reliable transport

- Can you produce/access enough seasonal produce to guarantee a delivery every week of the year? And make it look appetising? A winter box comprising solely of lumpy root vegetables won't tickle anyone's taste buds. What can you offer at this time of the year to keep your customers interested? Never be temped to supplement your stock with bought-in produce from wholesalers – customers will be able to tell the difference and you'll quickly loose their custom.

- It's the fresh, straight from the garden taste that makes the boxes so appealing. Can you include several different types of lettuce, and different sized tomatoes to add interest? Two large beefsteak tomatoes and a bunch of cherry tomatoes on the vine, for example.

- If including anything unfamiliar, such as kohlrabi, be prepared to include a Tip Sheet with information about the vegetable and a couple of suggestions for cooking, otherwise the produce will be wasted. Don't be afraid to offer something new or different, but make sure your customers know what to do with it.

- The advantage of the vegetable box scheme is that the contents have only been harvested one day before delivery, unlike supermarkets, which may keep produce in cold storage for days, weeks or months.

- It's better to convince a customer to sign up for the scheme in the late spring and summer when there is a much wider selection of fruit, salad and vegetables on offer. Possibly do all your planning during the winter, ready to launch the business in the spring.

- Think about your 'catchment area' and remember that you can't be delivering, gardening and marketing. What other human resources are at your disposal?

- Use standard sized cardboard boxes each week, and use bunches of herbs and vegetable leaves to make it attractive. Offer to remove the previous week's box when you deliver the new one but don't be tempted to recycle dirty or badly stained boxes.

- Prices generally begin around £10, and until you establish a small customer list don't be tempted to overreach your capacity for growing or obtaining fresh supplies. Once you're established, you can offer a deluxe box if your customers want something a little grander – and are willing to pay the extra money for it.

- When travelling around to introduce your service, make sure you take a few vegetable boxes made up to give people an idea of what they can expect. When the round is established, always carry a couple of extra boxes for potential customers who may want to buy them there and then.

- Don't be tempted to cover a wide area to start with – start small and gradually build up as your supply chains become more established. Start with a central location and work outwards, rather than picking areas at random which can involve a lot of driving and petrol consumption.

## Conclusion:

Check out any potential competition on the Internet and check other websites to see what they are offering their customers. There are nationwide vegetable box schemes in operation, so go on to their websites and see how they do things. Consider adding free-range eggs to the selection if you have access to local farm fresh eggs and including locally home-made jams and preserves to offer during the winter months. Include a weekly A5 recipe sheet with details of future selections.

# July: The flowering of the meadows

The popular television series, *The Good Life*, still has a lot to answer for when it comes to the lure of self-sufficiency. For many, the dream of a vegetable plot brimming over with Nature's bounty is only a fork's throw away. They see themselves serving freshly picked vegetables, fruit and salad to weekend guests, the pantry stocked with home-made preserves and pickles, and the freezer crammed with surplus produce to tide them though the winter (not to mention the new-laid eggs, home-reared lamb and goat's cheese...).

## The County Show & Game Fair

County Shows and Game Fairs attract people of all persuasions, for this is where they can meet sympathetic folk with communal interests and expertise. The County Shows are much more of a tourist attraction, but they provide a great day out with something for everyone, especially the writer. These events are often one of the highlights of the farmers' calendar where they can indulge themselves in the pleasures of the stock ring without the mucking out, and have a little tipple in the beer tent. They can inspect agricultural machinery they can't afford, and have a little tipple on the trade stand.

There are all sorts of local produce to sample, including local cheeses, sausages, home-made pies and pickles, with the 'Best of Show' often destined for the local butcher's slab come Christmas. "That was a problem," says one 'incomer'. "Our local butcher used to have a photograph on show of some magnificent beast, complete with rosettes and full pedigree, and tell us that this was to be our Christmas dinner! Keeping and showing sheep ourselves has made us less sentimental, but we still feel uncomfortable if the animal was known to us."

Despite the predominantly agricultural slant, the really big shows like the Bath & West, Royal Welsh, Royal Highland, the Royal Show, the Three Counties and the Irish National Ploughing Championships provide a most enjoyable day out for all the family. And even more localised events offer the opportunity to rub shoulders with local people in a party atmosphere that even the most persistent rain can't dampen.

Unlike the County Shows, however, the local Game Fair offers very little by way of a sop to tourism, being the province of traditional hunters, shooters and fishermen. This arcane world is where real country folk go to relax and if anyone doubts the popularity of field sports, they should make the effort to visit a CLA Game Fair. This is the UK's largest country sporting event and is always held in a beautiful setting, with shooting, fishing, gundogs, gamekeeping and falconry remaining the core elements of the show.

On a more local level the fair will be a one or two day affair somewhere between a County Show and village fete and often a lot more fun. "The mink hounds were billed as putting in an appearance," said one local. "The wagon backed into the area, the huntsmen turned out in royal blue with red gaiters, blew his horn and the hounds tumbled out on to the grass. That was the last we saw of them. They picked up a scent and hurtled out of the arena, out of the showground and disappeared completely. There was a lot of yelling and horn-blowing, but we never saw them again!"

Game fairs offer more of an opportunity to get closer and spend time with those who know more about country living than the sales personnel that man the trade stands at the County Shows. There are falconry displays (and the birds often clear off, too!) and ferret, lurcher and terrier racing where the family pet can enter for the princely sum of 50p, not to mention equestrian events for all levels and ages. For sheer entertainment for the whole family, the local Game Fair is an event not to be missed and who knows, you might just learn something to your advantage.

The shows provide more grist for the writers' mill and can offer opportunities across the board for articles and interviews. Most show reports will be written 'in-house' but if we keep our eyes peeled for some innovative idea on one of the side stands, there could be dozens of pieces to write about. We don't necessarily write from first-hand experience; we use other people's information to produce articles, profiles and interviews. The original idea for the following piece, for example, came from my partner, who is a 'man of Kent'…

## Life As It Is Lived: Cherry Ripe!

A summer harvest to be remembered comes from where gentle sea breezes blow inland from the English Channel across the orchards of Kent. The early morning sun has burned off the sea fret that crept inland overnight, and overhead the sky is a bright burnished blue. It's the time for the annual cherry picking and it seems that, almost by some mysterious telepathy, the Romany wagons begin arriving as they've done ever since we can remember – old lorries rubbing hubs with traditional horse-drawn painted caravans.

Kent has long been famous for its cherries, which have flourished there since Roman times. The wild cherry was listed by Aelfric (a Benedictine monk of Cerne Abbas) in his *Colloquy* as a native of Britain, but it is believed that the Romans introduced the cultivated variety, and that medieval monk-gardeners grafted more productive varieties on to the rootstock of the wild trees. In later times the fruit was taken to London to be sold in the city streets, where the cherry sellers cried their wares, and Samuel Pepys mentions buying cherries for his wife, in his famous *Diary* of the 1660s.

From the same period comes *Cherry Ripe*, a traditional English song with words by the poet Robert Herrick (1591–1674) – music added later by Charles Edward Horn (1786–1849) – which contains the well-known refrain of the cherry-sellers:

*Cherry ripe, cherry ripe,*
*Ripe I cry,*
*Full and fair ones*
*Come and buy.*
*Cherry ripe, cherry ripe,*
*Ripe I cry,*
*Full and fair ones*
*Come and buy.*

There is also an earlier poem by Thomas Campion (1567–1620) using the same title *Cherry Ripe*, which has other similarities and suggests that the sight of the cherry-sellers must have been a common one in the seventeenth century. The song became popular again during the First World War, and in more recent years was heard in the 1982 film *Victor/Victoria*, sung by Julie Andrews at her character's unsuccessful audition at a nightclub.

The fruit, bark and gum of the cherry trees were used to soothe irritating coughs, treat bronchial complaints and improve digestion. Crushed cherries, applied externally, were reputed to refresh tired skin and relieve migraines. According to the seventeenth-century apothecary and physician, Nicholas Culpeper, in his *Complete Herbal*, the gum dissolved in wine, "is good for a cold, cough and harseness of the throat; mendeth the colour in the face, sharpeneth the eyesight, provoketh appetite, and helpeth to break and expel the stone."

In the kitchen, the fruit was cooked, eaten raw or (pulped with the stones) made into wine. It was also used to make conserves and liqueur. In medieval times, cherries were picked when they were wine-red and eaten ultra-ripe... but we're not thinking about our cherry-stained history as the flat wagons trundle out to the orchards with the fruit pickers on board.

It doesn't matter in which direction we look, trees stand in regimented rows as far as the eye can see. These sweet cherries grow on magnificent full-standard trees planted some forty feet (12 m) apart, and the grass in between has been clipped short by grazing sheep. This is the most demanding of all fruit trees and can only be grown satisfactorily in the deep brick-earth soils largely found in Kent. Starlings and other fruit-eating birds flock from miles around, so cherries have to be grown in large enough numbers to justify various bird-scaring devices that the farmer has to employ as the fruit ripens.

Families are already out among the trees with baskets and the huge inverted V-shaped wooden ladders to begin stripping the ripe fruit from among the sheltering leaves. Local families work shoulder to shoulder with Romany families; the women wear brightly coloured headscarves as protection from the blistering rays from the sun.

Our noses and shoulders carry the white smear of calamine lotion to sooth yesterday's sunburn, as we wait at the bottom of the ladder to tip cherries into the big baskets that will earn the family its day's wages. It's hard work but all around there is a pervading sense of camaraderie and laughter. We break for a hasty lunch of thick salad sandwiches of fresh-picked tomatoes, crisp lettuce and the sharp tang of spring onions, all pulled straight from the garden earlier that morning. There's home-made lemonade and ginger beer for us children, while our mother pours a thick brew of tea from her battered cream thermos flask.

It's a long, hot afternoon ahead and we watch anxiously as the baskets seem a long way from being filled. The setting sun finally heralds the close of another day and it's almost dusk by the time we present our overflowing baskets for weighing. The Romany fires have been lit and mouth-watering smells follow us as we ride our bikes down the winding lane. Almost too tired to think about supper, we cycle home just as a sprinkling of stars begins appearing in the west.

There's an anonymous contemporary Romany poem on the Internet that just about sums up those memories:

*Fruit picking in the summer we always did in Kent,*
*In the cherry orchards was the best time that I've spent,*
*If I could go back in time, I know right where I'd be,*
*Sitting on a cherry box as my father played for me.*

A quick and economical supper that our mother often made from any leftover fruit was a cherry batter served with ice cream or custard. I was recently delighted to find a similar recipe in a 1930s edition of *The Woman's Treasury for Home & Garden*, discovered at a local car-boot sale: "The cherries were placed in a greased baking dish and sprinkled with caster sugar. They were then covered with batter (the kind used for Yorkshire pudding, but sweetened) and baked in the oven for 40 mins."

Just add the ice cream and step back in time…

**Published in the August 2011 issue of *The Countryman***

Here we have an article that is almost completely based on historical reflections, and a bit of family nostalgia, both linked to the traditional part the Romany played in the harvesting on Kent farms during the 1900s. Even the recipe is taken from a 1930s publication to give an old-fashioned feel to the piece – which might just as easily been written for *Evergreen* or *This England*. The idea stated when my partner was reminiscing about his childhood in Kent – I just picked up the ball and ran with it.

## Marketplace

'Good Life' magazines are more 'kitchen table than coffee table' and cater for those looking for a life of self-sufficiency; directing them towards realistic solutions with practical articles tailored towards the smaller acreage or large garden [i.e. *Home Farmer*, *Urban Farmer* (USA), *City Farmer*

**(Australia)].**

James Douglas writing in *Country Illustrated* observed:

> Perhaps the town dwellers, dismayed by the increasing speed at which the quality of urban life is deteriorating, yearn for the consolation of an unreal, dream-fulfilling countryside – a countryside which, alas, never existed, and never will exist, neither here nor anywhere else. Given the state of our towns, it would not be surprising if they did imagine rural England in this light.

And nowhere is this illusion better displayed than when those town dwellers visit friends who have moved to the country. In his book *Out of Your Townie Mind*, Richard Craze (an ex-townie himself) ruefully examined the pitfalls. For example, when we knew our friends in the city, we invariably met up with them for an evening; but the whole point about townie friends, once we have moved to the country, is that they stay for a whole weekend. "They suddenly seem very picky and faddy about food. They insist on seeing all the local tourist attractions, which you've visited every weekend since you moved. They mock you about moving to the sticks, instead of being suitably impressed. They seem bright and fun and young and you realise that living in the country has made you old-fashioned, out of touch and drab."

As Richard Craze goes on to observe, another classic mistake is imagining that because our environment changes, we will automatically change with it. It happens over and over again, where people imagine they will become proficient shooters, gardeners and enjoy tending livestock, only to discover that they have neither the time nor the inclination for gardening, sheep and chickens, or traipsing about over ploughed fields in the depths of winter for a pigeon shoot. Wherever we go we take our lifestyle with us, and if lack of time was a major problem in the town, it will still be a major problem in a village. In other words, we would be ill-advised to take on six acres of land, a major house renovation, or a horse unless we have time for it now!

On the other hand, a modest 'Good Life' living *can* be applied to our urban lifestyle, providing we curtail our activities to growing and cooking things, rather than trying to incorporate livestock into the equation. And we will still have plenty to write about that will interest other country and would-be country dwellers as we regularly explore local Farmers' Markets, Food Fairs and County Shows.

## Exercise: Submission Guidelines

*Q:* **Why do we have writers' submission guidelines?**
*A:* **To prevent everyone wasting their time in sending and receiving material that is totally unsuitable for that particular publisher or editor.**

Writers' guidelines *are* there for a purpose. They give the writer an overall idea of what a commissioning editor is willing to consider for publication – magazine or full-length book. Although they are usually quite comprehensive, a brief glance is no substitute for paying a visit to newsagents or bookshop to get an even better idea of the content, style and taboos for that particular market. The commissioning editor can always tell when the current editions of writers' handbooks have hit the shelves, because there is a marked increase in the number of totally unsuitable proposals and/or typescripts arriving in the post or by e-mail.

Writers' guidelines often state what commissioning editors *don't* want to receive – or what they are not prepared to consider, including whether they will accept submission by e-mail. Receiving material that blatantly flouts the guidelines is a source of irritation – just as much as receiving material from writers who have never even bothered to read a couple of issues of a magazine, or studied the backlist of titles and found the right imprint. Believe me, it *is* obvious.

Guidelines help professional writers to ascertain just *how* a commissioning editor wants to receive submissions and whether the initial idea can be *re-tailored to suit* the house style of that publisher or magazine. If an editor likes an idea, they *may* suggest an alternative because the sender has demonstrated a totally professional approach from the start. Under no circumstances will a commissioning editor consider books or articles that do not fit into their specified category. All commissioning editors are sent typescripts for children's books, poetry and other unsuitable projects largely because would-be authors haven't bothered to find out the basic requirements. **Items of this type are immediately rejected.**

By now we should have quite a collection of submission guidelines from a wide variety of publications, together with a copy of the relevant magazine. Keep these together in a large box file and update the magazines from time to time. This way we keep our eyes peeled for suitable outlets for our work. Remember that editors are constantly changing and each new editor will want to put their own 'stamp' on the publication – which may in turn provide a fresh market for the eagle-eyed writer. Spend at least one day a month on the Internet searching for new country magazines and book publishers, both at home and overseas, that might offer other opportunities.

# August: The height of the silly season

There are always fors and againsts as regards to living in a rural heartland, but one thing that can't compare is the natural beauty of unspoilt countryside, with each county having its own distinctive landscape. The air is undeniably cleaner and the environment usually much more relaxed than in the town. Food is also much fresher and often much cheaper if bought from a local Farmers' Market and this is the province of the regional publications.

## Don't Fence Me In

Nevertheless, one thing guaranteed to cause friction between country folk and incomers is a roaming dog – and for dogs used to an urban environment, a flock of sheep can be a tempting sight. Up to a few years ago gamekeepers and farmers shot roaming dogs on sight, but such drastic action would undoubtedly result in legal repercussions today. Farmers who shoot straying dogs now have to prove damage to livestock, and that they had no alternative but to kill the marauders. That said, a dog doesn't need to savage sheep to cause financial losses to a farmer. Sheep are hysterical animals at the best of times and a playful dog can cause ewes to abort or even die simply by chasing them. To the dog, with no malice aforethought, it may seem like a wonderful game, but it can turn out to be an extremely costly one for its owner.

Straying dogs don't have to worry livestock to cause a nuisance. A young sheepdog visited one local resident almost nightly, sitting beneath his window and howling. The moment it heard the back door open it scarpered – until the next night. By nefarious planning worthy of the SAS, the sheepdog was eventually captured and handed over to the local dog warden. The outcome was that the dog was claimed by a farmer who lived a couple of miles away – his excuse for the dog straying was that he couldn't keep it shut in at night because all it did was howl until the next morning!

Scamp, on the other hand, was more resourceful: a small, nippy fox terrier, the biggest difficulty was keeping him out. That little dog would scale walls and clamber in bathroom windows if the object of his desire was on the inside. Scamp was a local character and fathered more litters of puppies than any other dog in the neighbourhood until he was hit by a passing car while his mind was probably distracted by other things.

On a more serious note, taking an urban dog to the countryside can be a recipe for disaster if owners haven't made sure all the boundaries are secure. In a small community, owning a dog that isn't under proper control is not going to win any support from the neighbours – and neither are free-range children. It is also very important to keep children under control. Farmland is not a theme park or adventure playground; it is a place of work and there are dangers for those unfamiliar with the environment – but access to farmland is not a public right.

One of the quickest ways to fall out with a farmer is to allow both dogs and children to rampage over his land without first asking permission. Despite the accusations of groups representing the ramblers, walkers and hikers, farmers rarely object to local people walking across their land: what they do object to is the cavalier attitude of what they refer to as the 'boots and rucksack' brigade, who seem to think it is their 'right' to go where they please, irrespective of whether the land is private property or not, and to allow dogs to run loose among livestock.

"We've completely changed our attitudes to the 'right to roam' policy," explained one 'incomer' who moved to a local firm of solicitors from a large town. "When disputes appeared in the news, we'd always thought 'For goodness sake, what harm does it do?' but having a public footpath about 100 yards from our house has put a different slant on the subject. At weekends, from

April to September, we are regularly confronted by a posse of orange and blue anoraks who have got lost and have decided to use our garden and drive as a short cut back to the main road, even though there is no right of way."

"Sometimes it can be very creepy to have complete strangers lurking about when I'm at home on my own," added his wife. "It wouldn't be so bad if there was an apology but they seem to think it's their God-given right to trample over someone else's property without a 'by your leave', when they've no right to be there. I don't want strangers around when the children are outside playing, it makes me nervous."

Footpaths originate from tracks used by local people to take short cuts to neighbouring farms, villages, churches or places of work, but constant use over generations now makes them a public right of way. This means that the public has the right of access to use the footpath: it does not mean free-ranging over the field, or allowing dogs to run about off the lead. Bridle paths have a similar origin but are designated for the use of riders – and in the country referring to 'riding' means horses, not mountain bikes or any other form of mechanised transport! And never refer to 'horseback riding' because in the country there would be the response, "What *else* would you ride?"

Again, the writer needs to be aware of both sides of the argument when tackling emotive subjects like these... but there are ways and means of integrating them into our writing. For example:

## Life As It Is Lived: High Chaparral and Quince Jelly

This is the month of dog roses, honeysuckle and foxgloves in the hedgerows, with ox-eye daisies and rose-bay willow herb on the forgotten edges of the meadows.

It's been a very wet summer so far, and it's been a trying month to get the silage and hay under cover. Farmers have made hay since they learned how to combine the grazing of livestock with the cultivation of crops. It isn't possible, however, to just cut the grass and leave it in a heap in the corner and that's why we pay attention to the farming weather forecast. If the cut hay becomes really wet and stays wet, it starts to rot and the food value drops; if it is stored wet it will decompose. We started to cut our glorious hay meadows on the 10th and by the 16th it was safe in the barn while the weather still held.

We like to feed hay to the horses but our winter feed for cattle is silage. Here the cut grass is not dried completely and preserved by packing it together very tightly in a clamp to squeeze out all the air. The past two winters have been long and harsh and we're not taking any chances of running out of feed. We've taken two cuts already and the clamp is twice the size of last year, but we prefer to sell any surplus rather than having to buy-in food in at inflated prices in the New Year.

There's been a lot of humid, oppressive weather, sometimes with low cloud and drizzle off the mountains that does nothing to relieve the oppression, and towards the middle of the month it became showery followed by very heavy rain; with roads flooding, storm drains blocked and distant mountain streams gleaming white against the craggy green slopes.

We're not so weather dependent as we were but some things are firmly engrained in the countryman's psyche. Visitors have always been impressed by my ability to foretell rain but this comes from two things (and no doubt influenced by our geological surroundings). If it's a sunny day and the wind is coming in from the south-west, any rain clouds build up over a village some ten miles distant and take approximately 20 minutes to arrive. This means I've got the washing in and folded up before the rain starts to fall. If the wind is in the west, there is a distinct and sudden drop in temperature, which means the rain will be here in 5–10 minutes.

It's also been an endless trial of rescuing baby swallows from the kitchen window sills but there's something almost magical about holding one of these fragile birds in the palm of the hand. There's been a record number of fledglings here this year and every shady corner in barn, stable, shed and kennel has echoed to the cries of the parents on the wing, or babies clamouring to be fed. Each bird returns to the same nesting site year after year and we wait anxiously to see which birds have survived the long journey – aiming straight for the nest we've left from the previous summer.

Even the most hardened of countrymen will not harm a swallow. An old rural belief (which may appear as superstitious nonsense) holds that if a farmer destroys a nest or kills the bird, then his cows will yield bloody milk. This is, however, based on the fact that swallows feed on the flies that spread mastitis – a disease of cattle that tints milk red. An even older belief that was recorded in Saxon times said that with the arrival of winter, the birds submerged themselves into ponds, lakes and meres, from which they arose the following spring.

The quinces on the japonica tree outside the kitchen window are beginning to ripen and by October they will be ready to be made into quince jelly. In the spring the branches are covered with pale rose-coloured flowers, with the fruit forming like small pears. Quinces can be made into an unusual accompaniment for pork and cold meats, although the fruit is not eaten raw because of its astringent flavour and the hardness of its flesh. Quinces contain a large amount of pectin that makes them ideal for use in jams, jellies, marmalades, syrups, preserves and home-made wines; also cooked in pies and tarts with apples, pumpkins or marrow.

## RECIPE: Quince Jelly

*Quinces*
*Sugar*
*Water*

Wipe the fruit carefully. Do not peel but cut into quarters and put into a preserving pan with sufficient cold water to cover. Bring slowly to the boil and simmer gently until the fruit is tender. Strain through a scalded jelly bag – do not squeeze or the jelly will not be clear. Add 1 lb of sugar to each pint of juice and boil until setting point is reached. Test by taking a small amount on a wooden spoon and dropping on to a cold saucer. Pour into warm jars and allow to cool before sealing.

We're just about to have lunch when the phone goes. There's a slightly hysterical voice of the telephone engineer, who's marooned up his ladder surrounded by galloping cattle, and can we rescue him? Out into the lane and all we can see are loose cattle, hotly pursued by the horse, bucking and kicking with all the fun of the circus. From his vantage point the engineer tells us that two terriers are loose in the field and this is the cause of all the mayhem. Another hysterical voice can be heard high up on the ridge but the terriers are deaf to their owner's entreaties.

It's obvious what's happened. Someone from the nearby town has come out to exercise the dogs and they've run riot causing the bull and his harem to burst through the electric fencing, and career down the hill into the field where we keep the youngsters. The enlarged herd of cattle, pursued by the terriers, had ripped through another electric fence and the stampede joined by the horse – half ton animals galloping in all directions with yapping terriers at their heels. And a terrified telephone engineer desperately clinging to his pole, waiting for the ladder to be kicked away by a snorting bull.

At this point, and unable to contain themselves any longer, the greyhounds squeeze through the gate with the terriers firmly in their sights. By this time the terriers have decided that discretion is the better part of valour and, too terrified to yap, they head back towards their owner as if the very hounds of hell are on their trail. Fortunately they reach the tree line halfway up the slope and disappear into the undergrowth before the greyhounds reach them. No doubt the equally terrified owner was watching as our hounds closed in on their pets, but we'd little sympathy as we listened to the sound of slamming car doors and revving of the engine as the vehicle roared out of the Glen.

It was a miracle that nothing was injured and the only damage was the broken electric wire but there could have been thousands of pounds worth of destroyed stock – and all because some irresponsible dog owner can't keep a couple of terriers under control. The cattle and horse are eventually returned to their respective fields and the telephone engineer fed copious cups of sweet tea to help him overcome his ordeal – while the greyhounds were appeased with a Bonio apiece.

Harmony has been restored to the kitchen but it's too late for lunch and so we make do with a scratch meal of cheese and pickles. We're using the last jar of my home-made pickled onions, and these are given an extra 'zing' by using malt vinegar instead of the pale pickling variety – and a generous tablespoon of pickling spice. Nothing can beat the taste of home-made pickles and chutneys to serve with cold meat and cheese – and from now on the slightly under-ripe fruit and vegetables will be added to the store of preserves in the larder for use during the long winter months.

**Published in the August 2012 issue of** *The Countryman*

This article showed how the tranquility of the countryside can suddenly be shattered by an idiot dog owner, who doesn't think a small dog can do any harm among cattle. Agreed, the image of a desperate telephone engineer clinging to a pole, surrounded by galloping animals, *does* raise a smile but imagine the serious injury that *could* have been caused! Including the story among normal, everyday happenings takes the sting out of the tale, but it still makes the point.

## Marketplace

**Regional and county magazines are usually glossy monthly or quarterly publications featuring county events, entertainment, businesses and personality profiles of local people [i.e. *Welsh Country*, all County magazines, i.e. *Sussex Life, The County Magazine* (Somerset), *National Trust Magazine, The Dalesman, Dorset Magazine*, etc.].**

**County Living** and **County Life** – No, these are *not* the titles of new magazines – merely a way of drawing writers' attention to the fact that most counties do have their own glossy magazines that provide opportunities for freelance writers. Unfortunately the editors are often inundated with nostalgia pieces that are not in keeping with current editorial policies. As with all market outlets, the writer needs to keep a finger on the pulse of their target market, and it obviously helps if there is some strong connection with that particular county.

What county magazine editors are really looking for are profiles and interviews with people living and working in the region, especially if this can be connected to some current news event or local business development. Articles and features need to be entertaining, covering such diverse subjects as social events, art, fashion, county sports, antiques and motoring. Combine any of these with an interview with the organisers and/or participants and you might have something that has editor appeal. We should also keep a diary note of forthcoming Food Festivals that are held in large towns and cities to showcase the quality and diversity of local food producers.

Childhood memories are usually another no-go area unless they can be linked to some current news or event. Historical buildings have probably been done to death, too, but if you can come up with a new twist, the editor will consider it – unless a dozen other writers have come up with the same idea! Regional editors are no different or less professional than their urban counterparts, so let originality be your watch-word if you want to get into print.

## Exercise: It's Where You Do Your Shopping That Counts

Even if we don't have an interest in writing about farming, nature or wildlife, there are still quite a few topics that can be explored for a wide variety of country magazines. Items of community interest appeal to native and incomer alike, so again we learn to diversify and report on local news events. For example, in any country village the closure of the shop and Post Office can be disastrous, especially for the elderly and those without transport. Like the church, the pub or the parish magazine, it is a focal point of village life and the place where we make first contact with the locals.

Unfortunately, for those used to urban mega-stores, many village shops are considered to be behind the times; they don't stock goods or brands that incomers want and can be drastically overpriced. More and more, these small family concerns are being forced out of business simply because the turnover no longer covers the running costs. The shop and Post Office in a Wiltshire village found itself in such a position when the proprietor announced her retirement, but the villagers rallied round and formed a 'village shop association'. The shop's landlord made the magnanimous gesture of offering a five-year lease when he could possibly have sold the site for development.

This story, related in *The Daily Telegraph*, revealed that out of 300 people on the parish's electoral roll, 170 bought shares, while others pledged loans from £5 to £500, and within five weeks they had raised enough money to restock and redecorate. A handful of volunteers manned the counters on a regular basis and there is now a steady stream of customers going in and out. On top of the facelift, the chairman of the parish council applied to the **Countryside Agency** for funds from the **Vital Villages Scheme** and received a grant of £21,500 towards the venture. Other similar stories would appeal to most editors in the rural publications genre.

Agreed, the village shop may be more expensive and carry a smaller range of goods, but it pays in the long run to do at least part of our weekly shopping locally, even if it's only vegetables and meat from the farm shop and eggs from a neighbouring farmer. And if we live in a rural area without a shop or Post Office, or if they are being threatened with closure, it might be worth contacting **Rural Community Shops** (formerly ViRSA), a Dorset-based charity supported by the **Plunkett Foundation** which helps at "re-energising rural retail services". This organisation has helped more than 800 villages and has established about 40 community shops and Post Offices in England and Wales. They encourage local people to form village associations in order to buy or rent a property in order to run the shop and Post Offices themselves. They are now helping to support the survival of many threatened rural pubs too... so do your homework, contact these different organizations for some background information, and find some worthy subjects to write about.

# September: The return of the hunter

Not so many years ago there *was* a good-natured divide between the urban and rural communities. 'Townies' thought of us country dwellers as a bit on the slow side, while the 'swedes' looked on their urban cousins as a good audience for a tall story – especially over a pint in the village pub. The winds of political change have altered all that with 'town' and 'country' now sitting firmly on opposite sides of their respective fences. The destruction of the farming industry and the relentless erosion of rural autonomy *has* hardened the hearts of genuine countrymen and women, and this 'hardening' is reflected in the content of the publications which serve the rural communities.

## The Way We Were

Back in the 'good old days', when countryman Ian Niall wrote his regular column for *Country Life*, it was possible to reflect on the evocative images that were part of everyday life and enjoy the shared intimacy of the moment, encapsulated by Niall's pen. *Then* it was possible to talk about standing in a hide, deep in a wood, shooting wood pigeons fighting in at dusk. Listening and watching Nature getting ready for sleep, or awakening as the night approached, trees taking on new shapes in the lengthening shadows – a different feeling from the wood in daylight that cannot be put into words. There were the recognisable woodland sentries' warnings of a bedraggled and tired fox, with a big satisfied grin on his face, making his way home after eluding the local hounds... The sound of pheasants going to roost.

It is no longer *de rigueur* to write about duck flighting in January snow showers, with a biting wind and dark clouds scudding over a full moon as the hunter sits alone on the saltings with the tide rising to flood the river. Wondering whether the water will stop before it covers the little island on which we wait

– and even the dog looks worried until we hear the welcoming shout as the boat approaches at daybreak to take the hunters home for a hot bath, porridge, eggs and bacon and a large pot of tea.

These things have lost ground to more politically motivated issues, and those wishing to write for the 'real' country publications, i.e. those intended for the indigenous rural population, would be well advised to study the columns of RWF Poole in *Horse & Hound*, or Robin Page of *One Man and His Dog* fame rather than the feeble attempts of Germaine Greer and Ken Livingston!

We can't help but shudder at some of the things that are written, published and talked about today concerning country life by people who pretend to be country folk, just because they live in the country, have access to it, or own a four-wheel drive and a pair of green wellies. Many of these 'opinions' find their way into print because the person making them has political or celebrity status. For example, those belonging to the anti-hunt lobby who had on numerous occasions stated that they had no objection to animals such as badgers, foxes and deer being culled by using a *shotgun*. No countryman worth his salt would use such an ineffective firearm to dispatch an animal because the creature will die an excruciating death from lead poisoning – which is a much more cruel method than hunting with hounds. We know, we've seen the results.

Another misnomer that regularly finds its way into print (and fictionalised on television) is the accusation of class snobbery within the rural communities. This point was raised in a *Daily Telegraph* piece when a local man allegedly referred to "that lot on the council estate" in an article on the urbanisation of the Cotswolds. As a native complained afterwards, the quote was made by an 'incomer', and the naive journalist hadn't recognised the 'snobbery' as imported. Of course everything in the countryside isn't perfect. There are good farmers and there are some extremely bad ones – but the current climate classes *all* farmers as exploitative and mercenary when, in fact, the opposite is true.

Neither should the countryside be viewed with mawkish sentimentality, or as a giant theme park for the convenience of commuters and weekend visitors. It is the home and workplace of thousands of people who do not want to see their lifestyle vanish. There is still a small market for good, well-balanced journalism without it becoming swamped by politics. Magazines such as *Country Life, Horse & Hound, Farmers Weekly, The Field* and *Shooting Times & Country Magazine* will always be on the lookout for positive, upbeat material by knowledgeable writers capable of writing objectively about their subject.

**Published in the February 2000 issue of *The New Writer* for the 'Markets' section.**

## Life As It Is Lived: Autumn Equinox and Absent Friends

It's four o'clock in the morning, a few days before the Autumn Equinox, and one of the dogs is demanding to go out. Cursing under my breath, I fumble for slippers and dressing gown before stumbling downstairs. The morning air is crisp; there is a subtle lightening of the sky over the mountains and there... due south... is the constellation of Orion, palely loitering in the predawn skyscape. The hunter has returned and with him comes Sirius, not visible for a few more days, but still there, hidden by that predawn mist.

It's long been a family custom to say that our deceased greyhounds have gone to join Sirius, the Dog Star, and Orion must have acquired quite an impressive pack after all these years. The year before we'd added a very special, aptly named dog. Finn was aggressive... or as our friend at the rescue centre had described him 'of uncertain temperament'. With the silver-white hair of a Kentucky colonel, he was handsome, and he knew it, and as experienced greyhound people we decided to give him another chance.

As a sign of the times, there has been an increasing amount of theft from neighbouring farms, from chainsaws to cattle, and we'd been discussing the need for a guard dog as dog-theft was also rife in the area. We didn't need to look further – Finn had found gainful employment. The word went out that we had a ferocious guard-dog and no one was coming through those gates with him on patrol. Even neighbours who were regular visitors used the bell at the gate to announce their arrival rather than risk his wrath.

We never got to the bottom of the reason behind his aggression. His attitude to the other greyhounds was that of a regimental sergeant major. If they played up, he'd just loom over them with ears pricked and neck arched to convey the message: "Don't even think about it, son!" For all his aggressive posturing, however, *we* never ever felt afraid of him, or feared he might attack any of the family. A fearsome snarl was met with, "Oh, shut up, Finn!" and he'd just look offended before turning his back on us. The only fearful moment was the day we thought we'd lost him. It was a bitterly cold winter's afternoon and he wasn't anywhere to be found. We tramped the fields and hedgerows; we trudged through the woods, and along the riverbank, calling him. And if ever a dog had a near-death experience, it was hours later when, tearful and frozen to the bone, we returned home to find *him* snug and safe curled up in a nest of cushions in the sitting room!

Slowly he mellowed. He also led the community singing – something rarely heard outside a greyhound kennel. For those who have never heard greyhounds sing, this beautiful sound has an eerie, ethereal quality that makes the hairs on the back of the neck tingle. It's the sign of healthy, happy dogs and Finn was in charge.

The first sign of ill-health was the onset of pannus, an inflammatory condition of the eyes aggravated by sunlight, and a year later, a small lump on his nose was diagnosed as osteomyelitis, an infective process that encompasses all of the bone including the marrow, leading to bone sclerosis and deformity. After three different veterinary opinions, all we could do was wait as the growth got bigger and disfigured one side of his handsome head.

He continued to run with his chums every day, and was still fighting fit, but time was short and so he was allowed to sleep on the bed during the final months of his eighth year. One morning he walked into the surgery with tail wagging as he greeted the staff, before bravely presenting himself to the vet for that lethal injection. In the final second he turned his proud head to look at me and his eyes seemed to say: "Don't worry, it's okay. Catch up with you further down the line, eh?" and then he was gone. He'd given us four years of friendship and left a four-dog hole in our lives...

So, there I stood in the crispness of the early autumn morning with my hand on the collar of another old dog whose time was running out, watching and waiting. Finally I returned to bed, cold but happy. "Finn's back," I said to my sleeping partner.

Another harbinger of autumn is the departure of our swallows. Last year we waved off 40 or more as they gathered on the telephone wires but this year only three returned. With the cold, wet summer the insect level was down and our local country radio reported that both chicks and adults were dying because of the adverse weather conditions. We anxiously waited for our babies to fledge... and yesterday, we counted 19 from our little community gathering for that long flight.

All that will be left is the large amount of droppings in barns, garage and kennels that will require power-jet cleaning – and the deafening silence. Their chittering and chattering dominates the summer months, just as the song of the robin will rule the winter. We leave the nests *in situ*, even those in inconvenient places, because we feel that these birds deserve to find their homes intact *when* they return in the spring. And come the Spring

Equinox, we will start to scan the skies again for signs of 'our' swallows returning.

September usually brings the Hunter's Moon, the first full moon after the Autumn Equinox when meat stocks were set aside for the winter and cattle were culled to conserve food and fodder. The month is traditionally represented by the apple and the perfect time to combine the traditional elements in the form of a pork and apple casserole. Made from inexpensive cuts of pork, this can be served in the dish in which it is cooked to prove a substantial family lunch, or served as an informal supper dish.

## RECIPE: Pork & Apple Casserole

2 lb lean pork, boned
1 tablespoon butter, softened
2 medium sized onions, chopped
½ teaspoon dried sage
½ teaspoon salt
2 grindings of black pepper
2 medium sized cooking apples, peeled, cored and thinly sliced
3 tablespoons of water
1 ½ potatoes, peeled
2 tablespoons hot milk
1 tablespoon butter, cut into pieces.

Remove any excess fat from the pork and then cut into cubes. Grease a large ovenproof casserole with the butter. Put the onions, sage, salt and pepper into a mixing bowl and stir to mix. Into the casserole, place about one-third of the pork cubes and cover them with one-half of the onion mixture and with half of the sliced apples. Continue to fill the casserole with the remaining pork, onions and apples finishing with a layer of pork. Add the water. Cover the casserole and cook in the oven (Gas Mark 3, 170 C, 325 F) for 2–2 ½ hours or until the pork is tender. About 30 minutes before the pork is cooked, boil the potatoes and mash with the hot milk and butter. Spread over the pork and dot with pieces of butter.

Late September also brings a crop of crab apples that can be used to make Crab Apple Jelly. Most crab apples are about the size of a damson and sour to the taste, although there are those that turn a beautiful yellow with a crimson blush that are much sweeter. Crab Apple Jelly is an ideal accompaniment to roast pork, or alternatively the fruit can be used to make home-made wine. Old country recipes often say that the addition of a couple of crab apples make all the difference to an apple tart.

## RECIPE: Crab Apple Jelly

*4 lb crab apples*
*lemon peel or root ginger*
*Sugar*

Wash the apples and cut up without peeling or coring – just remove any bad portions. Barely cover with water (about 2–3 pints) and simmer with the chosen flavouring until tender and well mashed (about 1 hour). Strain through a scalded jelly bag. Bring the strained juice to the boil and test for pectin. Add the sugar (usually 1 lb sugar to every pint of juice). Stir to dissolve. Boil briskly till setting point is reached. Pour into heated jars and allow to cool before sealing.

Some people still like to call the Autumn Equinox the beginning of autumn, and although there is no official first calendar day for any of the seasons, the countryman will always feel the pull of the changing natural tides.

**Scheduled for publication in the September 2013 issue of The Countryman**

There is always a 'darker' element to autumn and it is reflected in this article about loss and return. Although the 'glorious Twelfth' signals the start of the shooting season, it's not until the following month that the traditional hunting season gets under way. This is the time when country people find the time to socialise after the long months of sowing and reaping... and even find time to have guests over for supper.

## Marketplace

**Hunting, shooting and fishing magazines usually have a workman-like approach to vermin control and catching food for the 'pot' or freezer [*The Countryman's Weekly, Shooting Gazette, The Shooting Times, Fieldsports Magazine, Game and Fish Magazine* (USA), *Gray's Sporting Journal* (USA), *Outdoor Canada, Hunting & Wildlife Magazine* (NZ)].**

The shooters' magazines cover all aspects of driven shooting both in the UK and abroad, including advice on gamekeeping, regular interviews with leading figures in the shooting industry, and reviews of new shotguns, shooting clothing and equipment. The gundog section offers advice on training and breeding, as well as reporting on gundog trials around the country.

Nature's bounty is given in many ways and country folk don't waste any of it. In fact there's an old country saying that the only thing that's wasted on a pig is its grunt. Similarly, if a local sees a pheasant hit by a passing car, he'll think nothing of stopping and picking up the casualty for his dinner. The unwritten rule is that it must be freshly killed and relatively undamaged; if it's been lying there for an hour or two, it will already have attracted other wildlife!

At one time no country kitchen was without rabbit on the menu at least once a week. Rabbits were introduced into the British Isles around the 12th century as a food source, and were originally kept in fenced enclosures. Today's wild rabbits are descended from the escapees from those former domesticated colonies, although *myxomatosis*, introduced in 1953, nearly wiped out the whole population, and many country folk haven't eaten rabbit since.

In some parts of the country it is not uncommon for deer to become road casualties, but here the unwary should think twice about visions of venison for the freezer. It may be that the carcass has lain there for some time. It may be that a vet had been called to deal with the injured animal and administered a lethal injection, the local kennels or abattoir not yet having arrived to remove the dead animal. Animals put to sleep by lethal injection cannot be fed to hounds as death would be inevitable and in such cases a vet should attach a label stating "Do not feed".

If the deer hasn't been killed outright, fear and pain would have increased the adrenalin pumping through its body; ruptured intestines could have resulted in toxins being absorbed into the flesh. A spokesman for *The Countryman's Weekly* advises that risking eating venison where the cause of death is unknown could have dire consequences. "Wasteful as it may seem, if you discover a dead roadside deer it is far wiser to notify the police or a hunt kennels. The best and safest venison comes from a beast killed by a stalker's bullet."

And last but not least, it's said that wherever we live we are never less than a few feet from a rat and, for most people, this creature produces the greatest fear after snakes. Rats were one of the few pests that private homeowners could have disposed of at public expense, although the fact that local authorities now charge for pest control is believed to account for the dramatic increase in the rat population. Homeowners are free to dispose of them however they wish, so long as no undue suffering is caused – such as 'catching them by the feet'!

Although mainly associated with urban areas, the brown rat also lives in open countryside in most parts of the British Isles. Many country rats make their way into farm buildings in winter and their presence can be detected by droppings or body smears produced by the greasy secretions of skin glands. Damage to food and the fabric of buildings is one reason why rats make uneasy bedfellows; another and perhaps more important reason is that they carry certain diseases, some of which are serious and even fatal to humans and domestic animals. Rats sniff around until they find a weak spot, such as a broken air vent in a ground floor wall or the gap plumbers always leave between the outlet pipe and the washing machine where the pipe pierces the exterior brickwork. So be on your guard against these unwelcome visitors.

## Exercise: Communication Problems

A large number of genuine country people *don't* hunt, shoot or fish – but their neighbours *do* and a lot of country social events orbit around these traditions. The barter system still survives in the rural heartlands and it's not uncommon for the shooter or fisherman to deliver a piece of venison or a couple of trout in exchange for new-laid eggs or milk from his non-hunting neighbour. Some farmers will not allow the 'field' to cross his land, only the hunt staff and hounds... but he'll still drink with the kennel huntsman in the pub and support the point-to-point meetings.

Obviously, things aren't as cut and dried as the writer might imagine, and we must not fall into the trap of assuming that non-involvement means disapproval. There were hundreds of what could have been seen as non-hunting people on the Countryside Marches prior to the hunting ban, simply because they saw their way of life as being under threat, and declared *against* the anti-hunting lobby in support of the countryside and everything it stood for.

Unless we have a thorough grounding in country matters, it's sensible to give politics a wide berth and stick to writing about what we know – until we learn more about what binds the rural communities together. Game recipes are popular with any of the sporting magazines so just because you don't approve of the activity, it doesn't mean you can't submit material for the sporting fraternity. Have you any old-fashioned recipes that would be suitable? Or a different way of preparing game? For example, the old country writers' chestnut of making sloe gin always had the addition of crushed barley sugar in our house.

# October: Trees ablaze with rich and varied colours

Whether we like it or not, hunting, shooting and fishing *are* an integral part of country life and, as we've already seen, often providing the only social activities available in rural areas. Enough has been said and written on the subject of hunting but suffice to say that this has been a traditional part of the countryside for hundreds of years. Regardless of which side of the debate we decide to take, it can only be stressed that it is a subject upon which opinion should not be over-ridden by either sentiment or ignorance of country ways. For example:

## Field Sports

Although not every one can afford to belong to an organised pheasant shoot, farmers and gamekeepers periodically issue an invitation to local shooting enthusiasts to 'man the coverts and flight woodpigeons' on a Saturday afternoon to help with the pest control. Our large population of woodpigeons is mainly resident, but some migrate to north-west Europe and migrants arrive in Britain during October and November to leave in March and April. A flock of pigeons can cause considerable damage on agricultural land as a single pigeon eats a handful of grain or seedlings a day, so a flock of 1,000 birds can strip acres of arable land in no time at all.

Despite the large flocks, woodpigeons are not easy targets especially, as when flying with a strong wind behind them, they can be exceeding some sixty miles per hour! As any pigeon shooter will explain, it is a much more exciting sport that other feathered game. Pigeons are canny and it takes hours of recon-naissance to reap rewards. It is also a sport in which every bird taken is eaten, either by the shooters themselves or via a local game dealer.

Before taking the moral high ground on any aspect of field sports we should remember that of the estimated **270,000** wild animals and birds slaughtered on the roads each year, the majority are killed by non-sporting people. Many aren't killed outright and are left to die an agonising death unless a passing sportsman stops and puts them out of their misery.

The following is an extract from an autobiography, ghost-written by myself, for field sporting personality Garrett Kelly – *Champagne & Slippers* – which is probably the most difficult thing I've ever had to write due to the fact that it had to be written completely from another person's perspective... and avoid the polemic style evident in the author's original notes.

### Life As It Is Lived: *Champagne & Slippers*
### – an autobiographical tale

Although there is much media hype over the exploitation of greyhounds and horses in coursing and racing, for me the animal's health and well-being have always been paramount. Horses and hounds are always linked in the countryman's mind and both have played an important, if dangerous, part in my life. With dogs, the danger is predominantly situated at the front end but with horses, the capacity for inflicting injury is far more global. Over the years, I have ridden out for some of the top names in National Hunt and Flat racing: Sir Mark Prescott Bt, Mark Tompkins, John Jenkins, Mark Johnston, Kate Milligan. Andy Crook, Patrick Haslam, Karl Burke, Kate Walton, Micky Hammond and Declan Daly – and I bear the scars from my time with them all.

Point-to-pointing and work-riding have always been my way of relaxing and keeping fit but, like all jockeys, I have constantly battled with my weight, existing on a diet of black coffee and cigarettes, or champagne and cigars when circumstances permitted. In the early days, Dad always kept a couple of point-to-point horses and, aged 16, I was qualifying them with the Enfield

Chase under the Mastership of Raymond Brooks-Ward. It was tremendous fun but in those days you were lucky if you encountered one fox in a season. Unfortunately, the point-to-point horses were always so fired up that you often found yourself on the receiving end of the Master's wrath for overtaking the field. In later years, I qualified Bill Cowling and Joe Rowntree's point-to-pointers with the York and Ainsty (North), so I experienced both sides of the hunting coin.

My weighing-in room companions in those good old amateur times were such good horsemen that they have all gone on to become professional racehorse trainers in their own right. David Kinsella, David Turner, Nigel Tutty, Tim Walford, William Wales, Don Cantillon... and now many of their sons are following in their fathers' footsteps. But as Clint Eastwood's character *Dirty Harry* has observed, "A man has to know his limitations," and my interests have always been firmly rooted in coursing: I would rather be a star on the coursing field than an also-ran in racing. This is not so bizarre as it sounds, since Sir Mark Prescott, although a leading racehorse trainer, has gone down on record as saying that he would rather have won a Waterloo Cup than the Derby.

In the days when I still had an active interest in both, the coursing crowd came along to Charm Park to watch me ride in a point-to-point race. I'd been briefed by Bill Cowling that he wanted Cult Figure in the middle of the field, but two of the jockeys had other ideas and closed the door. I took off between the horse's ears and made a face-down connection with the ground, ploughing a lone furrow with my hooter. My crash hat smashed into my nose and broke it for the fourth time. My coursing cronies cheered, but I was in the doghouse with Sir Mark Prescott for risking broken bones during the run-up to the Waterloo Cup.

That was not the first time that point-to-pointing might have jeopardised my slipping. Just prior to my sixth Waterloo Cup, I had come to grief while schooling my own horse, Balkash, with a view to riding him for the first time in a point-to-point at Higham. He screwed at an open ditch and left me dangling from the fence wings with two cracked ribs and the Anglia Cup meeting at Swaffham only days away. The Waterloo Cup Committee left me in no doubt that the stable door was to remain firmly bolted until the end of the coursing season.

Like dogs, horses have no respect for title or rank and I can well remember the venerable Brigadier Critchley, the National Coursing Club inspector, caught up in a tree during his judging days. He was a highly experienced old huntsman and point-to-point rider but his mount that day caused him to be unceremoniously hauled out of a tree in classic Mel Brooks-style. Dad was slipping a walked-up meeting at the Alresford Coursing Club and while the hare and hounds went off in one direction, the judge and horse made a beeline straight into an adjoining wood. There were sounds of cracking branches and pheasants flying, and the horse reappeared at a gallop, minus the Brigadier. He was a tough old bugger, however, and he continued the meeting strapped to the bonnet of a Land Rover, bouncing over the fields with only cushions between him and the metal rim of the spare wheel. The horse was taken back to Lambourn, snorting and bucking, to resume its racing career.

Anybody who has worked with animals for any length of time understands and accepts the very real risk of injury and accident. Working in close proximity to both the equine and canine during my 56 years has cost me dear in terms of scars and broken bones. I've broken my nose four times, and suffered three breaks to the collar-bones, cracked a wrist and an ankle, broken six ribs, dislocated a thumb, and had four front teeth knocked out, not to mention the subsequent violent removal of the bridgework. There was also a split thigh muscle, a ruptured spleen, and a missing finger.

Needless to say, dog bites were an occupational hazard and I normally got bitten anything up to 10 times a season. After one particularly vicious bite, I found myself at Epping Hospital in the presence of a formidable-looking Irish nursing sister who demanded I drop my breeches for a tetanus injection. Despite my pleas to have the needle in my arm, she insisted, and so I complied – to reveal a pair of women's tights. It is extremely difficult to explain that these items are a normal part of most sporting riders' attire, when you are face down in front of a woman brandishing a very large needle. All she said was, "Look, dear, what you do in your spare time is your concern. I'm only here to administer drugs."

I've also been stitched up (in medical terms) by the vet, the late Jimmy McWilliams, following a meeting at the Scottish National. The trainer of the gore-stained white greyhound, Charlie Frood, enquired where all the blood was coming from. I said, "It's okay, Charlie, it's mine." Whereupon he replied, "That's all right then," and strode off back to his van. The meeting recommenced and I found myself in the familiar position of having to drop my breeches behind the dog van, while the vet stuck a needle in my bum.

Among the old press cuttings is one from *The Journal*, dated January 21, 1980, which still makes me smile. "Garrett Kelly, a 29-year-old of Irish descent, his hands are knotted with unsightly scars – old and new – inflicted by excitable dogs that couldn't wait for the 'off'." And this was at 29. I wonder what he would think of the mess my hands are in now, with half a finger removed by a Suffolk Punch colt, and metal bars bolted to the bone in my thumb to stop it flapping about, the result of a previous riding injury.

Not all the injuries can be shrugged off quite so lightly; those six broken ribs puncturing a lung and rupturing my spleen led to the last rites being administered at St Margaret's Hospital, following a fall at Fakenham. Equally as spectacular, but less life threatening, was the car accident that could have cost me my sight. Leaving a Huntingdon Coursing Club meeting on route to the East of England meeting the next day, Bob Burdon watched me skid on mud at Elton and hit another car head-on, which put me through the windscreen, gathering glass in my right eye on the way. I was determined to slip the East of England and was forced to adopt the necessary affectation of wearing sunglasses and earning myself the sobriquet of 'Elton John'.

This catalogue of injury is not to demonstrate how tough I am; it is included to show the dedication of those who are committed to our sport and way of life. People such as my Newmarket chum, Declan Murphy, who, after a racing accident, spent six weeks in a coma but still rides out regularly for Mark Tompkins. Or the late Macer Gifford, who won two Whitbreads and rode in nine Grand Nationals despite his encroaching poor health. Or Ronnie Mills, who suffered a broken neck yet still rode to hounds and came back to judge countless Waterloo Cups. Or Bob Burdon, judging his second Waterloo Cup despite having to ride with one hand, the other so badly injured in a farming injury that it required skin grafts.

The ban on coursing under the Hunting Act 2005 has left us all with the strange sense of alienation in having witnessed the transition of a legitimate and ancient sporting activity, which has certainly been an integral part of my life, into one classed as a criminal pursuit.

**Extract published in the October 2006 issue of** *Country Illustrated*

This extract would not find favour with the majority of countryside publications even though it made very little reference to traditional coursing: but *Country Illustrated* ran it as a 5-page feature when the book was launched. Articles on field sports have a very limited editor appeal in today's country magazines, although as Sir Mark Prescott observed in his contribution to *Champagne & Slippers*: "In the 1920s [Garrett Kelly] would have been on the front of every cigarette card."

## Marketplace

**Rural publications cover community newsletters, local free newspapers and parish newsletters.**

If there are two things that are guaranteed to cause problems with incomers, it's the regular and liberal presence of sounds and smells that are normal, everyday occurrences in the countryside. Examples include the couple who bought a house next to the hunt kennels and then complained about the smell of cooking meat and baying hounds, or the chap who complained about the noise made by the local bikers, only to find out that the persistent roaring sounds came from the cattle in the field below his house.

You may also remember the case where an irate villager took an axe to the medieval door of the village church because she claimed she was 'being driven mad by the bell ringers'. From any potential housebuyer's point of view, if there is an old village church, then there are sure to be bells – and bell ringers. Bell ringing was a way of communicating news of a death to the community. It was generally accepted that until the 'passing bell' had been rung, the soul remained earthbound as it only "rose to heaven on the sound of the bell." This particular practice was stopped at the onset of WWII, when all the bells of England were silenced. For country people the sound of church bells on a summer's evening stirs pleasant memories of rural England and age-old traditions, but it might not be quite the romantic sound of bells across the meadows if you've chosen to live next door to the village church!

Animals, and livestock in particular, produce sounds and smells in large quantities. One farmer received a complaint about his sheep bleating when the lambs were sent to market. As he pointed out to the neighbour concerned, if her children were taken away she'd bleat for a while! Cows can also make the most alarming of noises. "One cow in the village was named 'the dinosaur' because it sounded like something out of *Jurassic Park* when her calves were taken away," remembered one village resident. Cockerels also come pretty high on the list when it comes to neighbour disputes, simply because they don't just crow at dawn – they crow whenever they feel like it.

Good, old-fashioned, organic muck-spreading is another bone of contention between the farming community and incomers. It's the cheapest and most natural of fertilisers and has to be transported from the farmyard to the fields by wagon, which means that the road through the village can be like an oil-slick until it dries off. It makes the most appalling smell for a few days (if you live downwind) and everyone and his dog treads the slurry into the houses – but it only happens a few times during the year. Even that most traditional of farming pursuits, haymaking, has been known to elicit its own share of complaints, because people object to the wisps of hay and silage blowing off the farm wagons and into gardens as they pass through the village. And it has not been unknown for the police to be called out to 'deal with' farmers working by floodlight trying to get hay or crops in before the weather breaks.

These are all normal occurrences in village and farm life. Contrary to popular opinion the countryside *is* a working environment, not a theme park. This is one reason why some folk would be better off moving to a coastal or market town rather than 'a place in the country'. And all these issues will be reflected in community newsletters and other rural publications to provide material for the writer.

## Exercise: Politics & Correctness

Local people are extremely protective of what they see as their heritage. For over 200 years the unspoilt village of Selborne in Hampshire had been regarded as one of the most beautiful in the country. That was until a local landowner, with a grant from DEFRA (often referred to locally as the Department for the

Eradication of Farming & Rural Affairs), began digging up parts of the village in order to 'improve' the landscape. *The Daily Telegraph* reported that this "environmental improvement involved mechanical diggers ripping chunks out of water meadows to create three man-made ponds in the name of biodiversity."

Neither will there be much *local* support for the concept of the '21st century village' like the one built in Cambridgeshire, which caters for those who want the 'villagey feel' without having to run the gauntlet of getting on with the locals. In this instance the locals objected to having an 'instant settlement' of 10,000 people plus a business park being built on a greenfield site. They managed to delay planning permission for twelve years before the first bulldozers went in, but 'progress' had its way in the end. As a result it is the residents of genuine Domesday villages, whose cottages jut out into country lanes, who have to suffer the commuter rat-runs.

Community newsletters, local free newspapers and parish newsletters are a non-stop source of current local gossip and politics that could be of interest to editors of much larger country and national publications. The key to this type of writing is the 'human-interest' angle, whereby local people affected by the proposed changes are asked for *their* opinions with a view to gathering support for the campaign. Sticking to the facts is essential, but try to find the most heart-rending viewpoint when looking for saleable material. And if we *personally* happen to be passionate about a particular issue, then the more prestigious the marketplace, the wider the support will be.

Country issues loom large in the political arena. The 'Hunting With Dogs' debate, for example, chalked up a total of 700 hours of Parliamentary time – while that allotted to debating the wars in Iraq *and* Afghanistan totalled a mere 63 hours! The outcome, as Sir Mark Prescott observed, was a finely tuned and honed Bill that resulted in it being legal for a dog to kill a rabbit, but illegal for it to kill a hare! The most current, and set to be a long-running debate, is the issue of the HS2 high speed rail-link between London and Birmingham, which is planned to destroy some of the loveliest countryside in the British Isles – just to cut 35 minutes off the travelling time. Use local opinion to add differing viewpoints to the article.

# November: Preparation for the cold, dark months ahead

Rural areas can be very inhospitable in winter, especially with fog, high winds, the damp, penetrating cold and roads that are often not gritted or cleared of snow, which can make travel an uncertainty. Therefore we need to understand the different ways there are of socialising on a *very* local level. The current economic climate means that there is little left in the wallet for outside entertainment, so we need to look at producing articles that reflect these harsh times and offer suggestions that will suit everyone's pocket.

## The Social Scene

Once the novelty has worn off, the countryside is more likely to be viewed as a cultural desert since there may be limited access to fashionable cafes, cinemas or theatre. Again, rural folk do as they have always done, and that is to make their own entertainment, although those working on the land have little time for leisure. Getting up early in the morning to see to the animals and going to bed after the last hay has been brought in at ten or eleven o'clock at night doesn't leave much time for socialising. There are, however, several rural traditions that incomers interfere with at their peril – although a writer's offer of support may go a long way.

## The pub

Patronage of the local hostelry is a must for anyone wishing to become part of the village community as this rural institution usually plays host to the local sports teams, and is where the locals congregate for pre-Sunday lunch drinks. "We've got two pubs in the village," commented one villager. "One has recently been refurbished and caters for incomers' tastes for what they think is good 'pub grub', while the other is rough and ready where local farm workers can call in for a quick pint and a pie. Although the latter hasn't been decorated for years, it always has a roaring log fire and the food is better and at a fraction of the price. And we can pop in with the dog to catch up on the local sporting gossip."

"We held our breath when new people took over the village pub," said another local from a different village. "The previous lot hadn't been what you might call obliging and the place was empty most nights. The new folk wanted a small restaurant as the wife was a chef, but they didn't sacrifice space for it and within a few weeks they'd attracted the cricket and darts team back and taken bookings for the annual club dinners. The food is good and not hellishly expensive but you need to book a table even midweek. They've put heart back into the pub and into the community."

The Countryside Agency has estimated that more than six pubs a week are closing, while others are being turned into restaurants. Unfortunately, a refurbishment rarely retains the character of the old pub and locals aren't welcome in their boots and work clothes, and neither are the dogs. Village pubs, like The Woolpack in *Emmerdale*, should remain the focal point for social-ising for everyone, but locals and incomers are rarely united in what they think makes for a good village pub. Plenty of scope for writers' material for the regional magazines, and which might even suit the food and drink trade's publications if we do our homework correctly.

## The church

This is still the heart of many villages and not because the community is particularly religious. In many instances the church plays host to the mothers' union, the youth club, baby and toddler groups, the harvest supper, and lunch or supper clubs for the elderly in the parish, as well as organising numerous fund-raising events for various local causes. Very often the people supporting these events, either by donating or buying, are rarely seen in the pews for Sunday service.

One couple were quite pleased about the way they'd given the vicar short shrift when he'd called just after they'd moved in. "We soon told him where to get off," said the husband proudly. "We don't go in for any of that religious nonsense." As it happened, the vicar organised most of the social events and, as a result, they were never invited to anything and were soon heard complaining that they were left out of things happening in the village.

By contrast, another incomer explained that although there was a difference of religious opinion (she was a Buddhist), she was nevertheless always willing to support his community activities. "The parish newsletter was always pushed through the door and we gave to the various projects he got up to raise funds for the church. We even attended the carol service one year and his face was a joy to see when we walked in. He never tried to push the religious question and often dropped in for coffee and a chat. We were invited to everything, even if it wasn't *our* cup of tea."

Rural vicars don't tend to be as thorny or crusading as their more urban colleagues, simply because it doesn't pay. A fly-on-the-wall television documentary about the 'protesting vicar' merely showed a man out of his depth in a country environment, and in the end he lost heart and resigned. Country parsons (as they used to be called) are a very special breed, and it may be a mistake to dismiss them out of hand just because you don't share their particular faith. And there's always the possibility of an article for the *Church Times* (or similar) if it happens to be a particularly forward-looking parish.

## The village hall

Every country person has fond memories of the village hall because at one time every activity in the area was focused on these peculiarly rural British institutions. This is where we came for the Saturday night dance, the baby welfare clinic and it also served as a meeting place for the local Cubs, Brownies, Guides and Scout troops. They provided the venue for family parties and wedding receptions, the local amateur dramatic society performed the annual pantomime there, and the youth club catered for sulky teenage girls who only went along for the records and the boys, not to learn macramé or to play ping-pong.

"Our village hall was quite primitive, but it provided us with a venue for a weekly dance," remembers one villager. "To give it a bit of atmosphere, the organisers would swop all the normal light bulbs for red and blue ones, and the source of the music was an ordinary record player, with everyone bringing the latest from their own personal collections. The hall consisted of one large room with a stage, two toilets and a back kitchen that often had stinging nettles growing through the floor. Oh, the good old days!"

Unfortunately, with the shift in local facilities and entertainment, village halls have been in decline for years, with no local funding available for repairs and modernisation. As a result, most are musty, hard to clean, almost impossible to heat and incredibly barracks-like in appearance, but they still represent the social heart of many rural communities. They can also provide plenty of nostalgia for country magazines in addition to reporting on any unusual activities for community publications and regional newspapers.

## The village school

Those who went to village schools often received a broader education than many of their urban contemporaries, despite there only being a couple of teachers trying to cater for forty or so pupils of all different ages. As well as the normal schooling there were practical nature walks, the school band and choir, basic French, beekeeping, country dancing, the annual sports day and participation in the local fete. The pupils came from all social backgrounds and the teaching disciplines set the classless structure for village life, where the offspring from the 'big house' grew up to play cricket and hunt with the children of the local butcher. Few 'wealthy' children went to private school until they reached eleven years of age.

Unfortunately, many of these village schools have closed, and as a result, the community spirit is no longer nurtured in the classroom, simply because children often have to travel miles by bus for schooling, or are dropped at the gates by the 'milk-run' mums. It also means that children form friendships with others who live much further afield rather than those from the same village.

"Although my friend and I had completely different family interests, we lived in the same village and were inseparable for the first 15 years of our lives," said a native. "She stayed behind in the village and worked locally, while I went off to London. We're now in our 60s, but we still regularly keep in touch even though we now have very little in common apart from those roots, but they go very, *very* deep."

Many village schools have been sold for conversion to private homes, but those that do remain open still offer a community meeting place for those who live in the area, often replacing the function of the village hall. "The heart went out of the place when they closed the school," said one farmer whose yard is situated in the middle of the village next to the school. "The whole village felt as if it had died when the children's voices weren't heard in the playground any more."

Which is why there is always a strong campaign against the closure of a village school, and you'll win quite a few brownie points if you support the protest, even if you don't have children attending the school. Again the human-interest element can also provide articles for educational and parenting magazines, as well as regional newspapers.

## The Women's Institute

Often mocked and the butt of many cruel jokes, we should never underestimate the power of the local Women's Institute – after all, these are the ladies who dealt Tony Blair such a well-mannered blow when he tried to inveigle them in his politics. This well-publicised event demonstrated to the world at large that the WI wasn't just about ladies in twinsets and pearls arranging flowers and making jam.

The first WI was founded in 1897 from the ideas of Adelaide Hoodless so that women could enjoy similar educational and social advantages to those given to the men at the Farmers' Institute. The original WIs were based exclusively in rural areas and through close community ties and wide-ranging activities, the organisation has played a unique role. With a current membership of around 220,000, the National Federation of Women's Institutes is an educational, social, non-political and non-sectarian organisation that offers local women the opportunity for learning, campaigning and friendship – and not just in the traditional interests such as arts and crafts, but also in the latest developments in IT, health, fitness and science. The WI also offers the opportunity to play an active part in the community and make friends through social, practical and leisure activities. Prior experience of committee work, fund-raising, public speaking and social issues can lead to new members eventually taking a more effective part in community life.

During its long history, the WI has also undertaken a large number of valuable localised publishing ventures, which have preserved regional history, recipes and folk customs for posterity. Catering for the growing interest in local history, there probably isn't a rural Post Office in the country that doesn't sport a collection of illustrated guides to various towns and villages or postcards of historical buildings in the parish, many sponsored by the WI and then, of course, there was *that* calendar. *WI Life* is the members' magazine published eight times a year and contains articles on a wide range of subjects with a 'strong environmental country slant' including crafts, cookery and gardening – and not forgetting the country coffee-table glossies as a target market for similar types of articles.

Needless to say, it is inadvisable to write about country matters haloed with a rosy glow, since editors of rural magazines know better. As with everything in life, we need to be able to write with an eye and ear on both sides of any argument...

## Life As It Is Lived: Owl-Light and Street Lights

It's midnight in the depths of the countryside and the only sounds to be heard are the distant bleat of a sheep, the rushing of a nearby stream and the occasional hoot from an owl as it hunts along the field margin. The dog paces about nervously listening to the strange sounds made by the wind in the trees. If you are nervous of staying alone in a remote cottage miles from the nearest neighbour and with only the dog for company, then don't be tempted by the glamour of whitewashed stonewalls and the song of a skylark. By the time it comes to alter the clocks it will be a different world entirely and one that can appear hostile and threatening to those not used to isolation.

Because not all winter days are bright sunlight and crisp frost. Mostly our days are damp and gloomy with pale skies, heavy cloud formations, and often a rawness that makes us want to stoke up the Rayburn and pile logs on the fire. If we don't need to go out, then the weather gives a perfectly good excuse to stay indoors, but because we have livestock depending on us for their feed and exercise, the luxury of a warm kitchen has to wait.

It's always colder in the countryside than it is in the town, simply because the rural landscape isn't broken up by high-rise buildings, and the biting winds get a clear run at the front door! In Wales, we lived halfway up the valley, and when the westerly gales came in off the Irish Sea, there was nothing between the coast and the side of our house. Mind you, it had been standing for well over three hundred years so we took the attitude that it would probably last a bit longer, but during the gales we used to lie in bed and wait for the roof to come off, or for the chimney to come crashing down.

In the depths of a country winter all sorts of calamities can happen and the wise should always be prepared. One year the power lines came down and the snow was too deep for the electricity engineers to get across the fields to find the fault. The village was cut off completely for five days without light – and warmth, if you were reliant on central heating. That's why the locals all stuck to our battered Rayburns and open fires, stocked up the pantries, brought livestock close to the house and threw another dog on the bed. Quite a few incomers learned a lesson that winter, I can tell you!

Most properties that are over seventy years old will probably have played host to the Grim Reaper at some time or another, but there's nothing quite like the sounds which emanate from an old country cottage during the dark winter nights. Mention this to the woman who runs the Post Office, and in no time at all you will be told that the place is haunted by old Ben, or Bob, or Walter. Old buildings naturally creak and groan as the buildings heat up or cool down, and very often weird happenings can occur because of the structure of the land on which your house is built. We know that there is a grid of underground streams and watercourses that criss-cross the entire landscape, and these can produce enough natural sound effects to convince you of your own Amityville Horror.

Dozens of homeowners are now paying considerable amounts of money to have their homes dowsed, feng shuied, and cleansed in order to rid themselves of what they see as 'negative energy'. Very often those undertaking this contemporary form of exorcism arrive in an expensive car with personalised number plates and blind their clients with an arcane science relating to 'geopathic stress lines'. What those who genuinely work with such energies will tell us is that these pockets or lines of natural energy have a habit of moving around. It's highly possible that the energy flow will be due to the natural geological environment and there's very little anyone can do to 'cure' it. So if you've just paid out a fortune to have metal rods hammered into your lawn to interrupt the 'negative slurry', it could have headed off in another direction before the bank has cleared the cheque.

Dowsing is a genuine old country craft and just about anyone can do it using either two wire rods made from a metal coat-hanger, or the more traditional hazel twigs. Often used in the country to locate underground springs over which to sink a well, dowsing rods (or a pendulum) will locate just about anything from underground streams and buried metal, to ley lines and psychic disturbance! In fact, even in the construction industry dowsing for water or hidden cables is a 'reasonably well-known practice'.

Dr Ted Nield of the Geological Society of London said, "There is no known scientific basis for notions of so-called 'geopathic stress'. It is a concept more akin to ley lines and natural magic than any definable force, though it is a convenient means of parting gullible people from their money. The geological environment can affect humans – and sometimes not for the good. If you live in certain areas of the country, for example, you might have to be careful about radon in unventilated spaces. Some upland peoples used to suffer from iodine deficiency as a result of their local geology. The chemistry of the water you drink leaves distinct traces in your bones. But nowadays, with modern water supplies, this natural variation is never harmful."

That's official, so if you were thinking about calling in the 'experts', make yourself a set of dowsing rods and/or a pendulum and save yourself some money.

And no mention of long winter nights would be complete without reflecting on the 'street light' debate. In one village 75% of the local people voted against street lighting, simply because the light from roads, cities, streetlamps and airports are making it impossible to enjoy the night sky. In fact, there is so much light pollution in Britain that during the last eclipse of the moon, 80% of amateur astronomers reported that they couldn't even see the neighbouring stars in the Milky Way from their homes. Unfortunately for those campaigning to reduce light pollution, the problem has crept up so stealthily that those without a vested interest in the subject have failed to notice its scale and seriousness.

"I moved from Ireland to the Midlands to work," said one visiting local girl, "and for me the worst thing about an urban environment is the horrible orange fog that spreads across the sky, blotting out the stars. I used to love watching the stars come out of an evening when I was at home, but here I'm lucky if I can make out the brightest ones."

Sir Martin Rees, a Cambridge professor and the Astronomer Royal, used an ornithological analogy to highlight the problem. "I don't think you have to be interested in bird watching to understand that we would all miss songbirds if they were not in our gardens. The night sky is part of our environment and we must be concerned not to degrade it, just as we are concerned not to degrade our landscape. You shouldn't have to go to a remote part of Scotland to see the stars."

One countryman, who certainly wishes to remain anonymous, gave his viewpoint over a pint in the local pub. "For some reason best known to themselves, the local council replaced the old street lamp on the village green with an awful orange light. It's always broken because every time the council replaces the bulb, one of the lads takes his rifle and shoots it out to stop the horrible orange glare from shining into the surrounding houses. It's better for everyone without it but no one ever asked if we wanted the bloody thing in the first place!"

**An extract from *Signposts For Country Living*, published in 2010**

This piece has a tongue in cheek element to it but also offers a few serious 'warnings' about the downside of living in the country. The landscape *does* take on an eerie quality after dark and my partner positively hates dusk or 'owl-light', which he still considers to be spooky even though he's lived in the country all his life.

## Marketplace

**Equine and rural sporting magazines often provide an overlap between rural and urban readers [*Horse & Hound, Pony Club News* (USA), *Lakeland Walker, Country Walking, Hill Walking Magazine, Camping Magazine, Outsider Magazine* (Ireland), *Backpacker* (USA), *Go Camping* (Australia)].**

Rural people don't have a lot of superfluous time for socialising, simply because they are too busy working on the land or, if they do take time *off*, it is usually spent engaged in field sports – or some other allied pastime. Leisure is strongly linked to the 'day job' and writers learning about country pursuits discover that here is where the dividing line between town and country is often at its broadest.

By and large countrymen are by nature a hardy bunch who can endure the harshest of conditions in pursuit of their chosen sport. They work hard and play hard, sustaining the most appalling injuries while going about their business. Rural wives get used to having their men brought home in the back of a Land Rover, battered, bruised, broken and covered in mud after a skirmish on the hunting or rugby field. In the country this is all part of life's rich tapestry, and so is appearing in the pub the next day, battered, bruised and broken, but minus the mud.

Action men are the first to laugh at themselves and the painful predicaments they find themselves in and, by and large, have extremely high pain thresholds, which any incomer would be hard pressed to match. So, if contemplating writing about any rural action man pursuits, don't expect to see any sympathy in times of injury – they learn to grin and bear it. And provide plenty of opportunities for the writer who can produce humour for sporting or country magazines.

## Keeping an eye on the ball

Rugby and football have a keen following in the country, and are more than likely to have the supporters' club based in the village pub. Local leagues are taken very seriously indeed, but forget about the neatnesses of urban clubs and municipal pitches. In the country the pitch is the corner of some windswept field and, apart from the players and a handful of diehard supporters, the only other spectators will be a herd of cows and a bored dog, all of whom will invade the pitch just as the local striker is about to score.

By half-time the pitch will resemble the Somme as the teams, by now completely indistinguishable from each other, wallow hock-deep in mud. Some clubs have their own clubhouse complete with bath, but in most cases the end of the game is heralded by a wide assortment of hairy bottoms and jockstraps being exposed in the car park. This is rural sport at its finest and wives who have any sense simply leave them to it; show too much interest and they could be the one putting umpteen sets of mud-caked kit through their washing machine.

## The Answer's a Horse

It must be obvious to any writer that a considerable amount of country socialising revolves around horses, and that hunting still forms an integral part of those equestrian pursuits. As Serena Soames points out, "The Pony Club is an institution that fosters independence and confidence in children. It grew out of the hunting umbrella, so that children should learn to ride well enough to be able to ride to hounds. The hunting field is used to refresh stale competition horses; it is a training ground for point-to-pointers and steeplechasers; it is a nursery for most of the steeplechase jockeys riding in Britain and provides a second career for competition horses that have peaked."

A large number of social events in rural areas are arranged by the hunt members and can range from muddy treasure hunts to highly sophisticated dinners, and include people from all walks of life. In the country the horse is still king and it's the equestrian events that draw another dividing line between those from the country and those *of* the country, especially point-to-pointing. Point-to-point racing is another of those peculiarly rural activities that, up until recently, offered little attraction for those not born and bred to standing about in muddy fields for hours on end in the cold and wet. In more recent years, however, point-to-point has been attracting a much wider audience despite the sport's hunting associations, simply because it offers a chance to watch highly competitive racing fixtures.

Run by enthusiastic amateurs as fund-raisers, even the most experienced of riders can find themselves volunteering for the job of car park attendant, race-card seller, timekeeper, announcer, commentator, steward or, the most thankless task of all, judge. The races are run under strict rules and competitors must hold a Rider's Qualification Certificate issued by the Jockey Club, and are only eligible if they are members of a hunt. All horses running in point-to-points need to have been registered at birth by Wetherbys, and to hold a passport showing details of their birth and parentage. In addition, the horse has to be 'regularly and fairly hunted', after which the Master will sign and issue a Hunter Certificate.

Originally run straight across country (hence the name), these races are now conducted on official tracks with purpose-built fences, usually on farmland belonging to a member of the hunt. There are about 120 courses throughout the British Isles with the form and results being closely followed by the supporters. This is a day for stocking up the 'boot' of the 4X4 with plenty of warming food and drink and going with the intention of placing a few bob on who you think will be the winner.

Also organised by the local hunt, another of the most challenging of equine sports is team chasing, which is almost as thrilling for spectators as it is for the participants. Team chasing as a recognized sport is less than 30 years old, but considered to be one of the equestrian world's most exhilarating pastimes. Anyone can take part, but it is impossible to overlook the very obvious ties to hunting (ban or no ban), since most of the riders and spectators will be members or followers of the local hunt.

The event has been modified from the original 'natural' obstacles, but the ride is still not for the faint-hearted. A *Daily Telegraph* 'Weekend' report observed that "team chasing is a sport for those who abhor the nanny state with its preoccupation with 'health & safety'. Few back-protectors are in sight (compulsory in eventing), while there are no barriers or ropes behind which the spectators must stand." As an extension of the hunting scene, the social aspect of team chasing is as important as the actual participation, and the teams usually ride under such incongruous names as Feisty Fillies, Stroppy Mares and Three Old Farts and a Tart. Here there's no battle of the sexes, since both are more than adept at trading the most colourful and vicious of insults but, unlike urban and professional sportspeople, no one takes offense.

## The cricket club

One pastime where participants are *not* expected to risk life and limb is village cricket, which is a long way removed from the commercial politics and pastel jumpsuits of the Oval. In fact, as Tim Head of the *Telegraph* observed, in village cricket the game still survives in a form that would be recognisable to WG Grace and his brothers. "And is there still honey for tea? Well yes, actually, and it's a good strong sweet brew from the same huge tin or enamel teapots they used 100 years ago, or even earlier."

Of all the rural traditions, village cricket is the one that can still attract budding youngsters who may not find a place in the school team, a veritable army of tea-ladies, muscular farm workers and vicars in mufti. Unlike the rugby or football pitch, the cricket pitch is usually an immaculately kept rectangle of green in the middle of a cow pasture, and those in the position of 'fielders' spend a considerable amount of time rummaging around to retrieve the ball from cowpats.

But the village cricket season offers more than just a way of spending a pleasant afternoon lolling about in a deckchair and listening to the sound of leather on willow. The teams are often desperately short of players, particularly around the time of haymaking and harvest, and incomers who casually volunteer to 'make up the numbers if you need me' will quickly be absorbed into village life. The beauty of village cricket is that you don't have to be good at it, although it helps. One recently arrived fellow was watching a game and suddenly found himself enlisted for the following weekend, despite the fact that he hadn't held a cricket ball since he was at school. "A few games into the season and we'd been invited to all sorts of cricket 'dos' which we wouldn't have known anything about if I hadn't agreed to play. It doesn't matter if you're 'out' with the first ball, you're part of the team and no one cares, but it is the best way to get to know people, although my wife has yet to agree to help with the teas."

There are, of course, numerous other outdoor activities catered for in the country and a growing number of farmhouses and B&Bs that cater for walkers, especially in areas of outstanding natural beauty; while caravan and camping sites can be found in all sorts of locations. Articles featuring unusual or outstanding holiday venues could appeal to holiday/travel publications, as well as farmers' magazines where the readers could learn how others of their kind have diversified into the 'leisure' market.

## Exercise: Humour

As we can see, rural sporting and social events can provide the writer with numerous anecdotes to add the spice of laughter to an article – or for the 'sports widow' an article in its own right. The important thing to bear in mind, however, is that country humour is particularly non-PC... and often revolves around what is perceived to be the village idiot.

It's a good, politically incorrect topic, but every village has one, and they are not half as daft as they like to appear, like the story of the simple Welsh lad who hung around a film crew who were staying at the local pub. The director announced that he needed a dead fox for the next day's shooting and could anyone help. The lad piped up that he could provide the necessary body and the fee was agreed at £25. Next morning the dead fox was duly delivered and at the end of the day the lad was required to get rid of it. Some hours later the director turned up on the doorstep and explained that the scene needed to be shot again and that he'd need another fox. The lad scratched his head but allowed himself to be persuaded to obtain another for a further fee of £25. The fox was duly delivered and at the end the lad again disposed of it, as requested.

The director decided that he could use a fox in yet another shot, so he approached the lad again, but this time the price had gone up to £50 due to the growing shortage of foxes in the locality. What the film director didn't know was that the lad had remembered seeing a roadkill, which he had dumped in his mother's freezer overnight, fluffing up the fur with her hair dryer the next morning. At the end of filming the location sequence, over a pint in the pub, the film director made some comment about the lad being a bit simple. "Oh, I dunno about that," said the Welshman standing next to him. "He's made a hundred quid selling you the same dead fox three times over, so he can't be that daft, can he?"

Humour is a very personal thing and often falls flat because it is contrived, rather than depending on a graphic turn of phrase or the thumbnail sketch of a ludicrous situation. Writing humorous material must never appear malicious or spiteful, and very often the butt of the country joke is one person thinking someone else is stupid. Good humour is acceptable to any editor, so don't be afraid to try your hand at this style of writing if the right story presents itself.

# December: The time of the Midwinter Festival

Regardless of the subject or type of magazine, it is almost impossible to escape 'the Christmas issue'. In fact, it's difficult to avoid any seasonal theme throughout the year (regardless of what part of the world we live), and the indispensable reference book for any writer is the Chambers *Book of Days* (or similar), which gives an annual diary of events both ancient and modern.

Originally published in 1864 and described as "A Miscellany of Popular Antiquities in Connection with the Calendar, including Anecdote, Biography, and History, Curiosities of Literature, and Oddities of Human Life and Character", this Victorian compilation (together with a pad of 'post-it' notes) remains one of the greatest aids for the seasonal writer. Other parts of the world will have their own equivalent and can be used in exactly the same way.

## Plotting and Planning

Just like the farmer, 'plan ahead' should also be the motto of the country writer. Using our chosen 'calendar' for reference, by December we should be thinking about submitting seasonal material for June or September, depending on whether we are aiming at monthly or quarterly publications. If we wait until December to submit articles for Easter, the editorial boat will have set sail without us for the coming year!

Always keep a note of what you have submitted, when it was sent, and to which magazine. Create a 'submissions diary' for instant reference that also gives date of acceptance/rejection, fee (if any) and the publication date. It's always a good idea to keep a note of the current editor's name, and bear in mind that while some editors have been at the helm since Noah built the Ark, the majority change every couple of years. Editorial requirements change with the incoming editor, who will want to impose their own personality on the magazine, and that may alter the whole slant of what will be required in future, so keep up to date with editorial changes.

Unfortunately, it's becoming more and more usual for editors to sit on unsolicited articles indefinitely, and recently I've had two responses from completely different monthly magazines where the editor states: *"I'll keep this on file in case I want to use it in the future."* Sorry... no! If an editor hasn't responded within a month, then the article is revamped and submitted elsewhere. There's no point in waiting around while an editor hedges his (or her) bets, as the piece will be out of date if we have to wait six months for them to make up their mind. Having said that, the editor of *The Countryman* explained that he was working nearly 12-months ahead, and would I mind if my article was held back for publication until the autumn issue. Of course not...

A good magazine editor knows exactly what they want for the readership and should be able to make a decision reasonably quickly. This is why it's better to send a proposal letter or e-mail outlining the subject matter, intended approach and the reason why you are 'qualified' to write about it, but even if an editor likes your work and you write for them regularly, don't allow yourself to become complacent. Keep sending material to other outlets because you never know when there will be a change of editor – and the new one might want to make changes that don't include you!

Needless to say, every magazine has its very own style and a writer needs to be mindful of the subtle differences that make a *reader* prefer one weekly magazine to another. An article tailored for and rejected by one publication will need some tinkering before it is sent off to another – although on first reading both magazines appear to be almost identical. And do resist the urge to carpet-bomb all country magazines with the same article – it doesn't work that way.

Always make a point of mentioning a fee when submitting, i.e. *"I enclose my article for consideration at your usual fee..."* This tells the editor that you expect to be paid for your work. And it wouldn't be the first time I'd had a very prompt response stating that the magazine doesn't pay for contributions. Some editors state quite openly that it can take between 3–6 months before they will give a decision, so what are our options?

- All submissions should be tailor-made for the appropriate market and shouldn't automatically suit another editor's requirements. All typescripts would need some tinkering before being sent to another editor, so simultaneous submissions are not a good idea from the writer's point of view.
- By rule of thumb, give short stories, poems and articles a month before offering them elsewhere. Novels and non-fiction book proposals should be given between six to eight weeks before sending them off to the next publisher/agent on your list. Give them the courtesy of another six weeks to respond.
- A 'perhaps' 'later' 'maybe' response is no good to a writer. Keep your options open by all means, but a piece isn't sold until you have a formal confirmation.

The 'no simultaneous submissions' rule was put in place over a decade ago by editors, and has become another of those urban myths within the creative writing industry. It's dog in the manger stuff and if you've been waiting for weeks, or even months, for a reply, then it's hardly 'simultaneous' if you decide to submit to someone else after a reasonable delay. If your submission is accepted, do send a polite letter to any editor who's 'kept it on file' and explain that the piece has now been sold. And thank them for their time. You never know when you want to submit to them again.

## Life As It Is Lived: The Pagan Elements

The Winter Solstice, or the Mid-Winter Festival, is represented by the holly, symbol of the winter aspect of the pagan Holly King; the tree having been a decoration at the Yule festival for centuries, as it was used for the same purpose at the Roman Saturnalia.

In the depths of winter often the only greenery to be seen is that of the holly – and the ivy, clinging to trees, old walls and farm buildings, providing shelter for hibernating insects. Among the flowering disks, the insects can feed on the rich supplies of nectar, which is a rare thing at this desolate time of the year. According to one source, this sweet liquid can be so intoxicating that if the ivy is shaken, drunken insects will fall to the ground. Through January and February, the small green berries will mature, ripening into black fruits in the spring. As a result of all this insect activity, in mid-winter you will see a wide variety of birds poking around amongst the leaves.

On patches of bare ground and along the edges of fields where the grass is short, evidence can be found of rabbit scrapes. These small, horseshoe-shaped holes are an inch or more deep and show where the rabbits have been digging for succulent roots as part of their winter diet. This is the time of short days and long, dark nights although we can be sure to witness some spectacular sunrises and sunsets as the sun's rays tinge the frosty landscape a delicate pink. The low sun casts squat shadows along the hedgerow, while deep in the woods there is a frozen stillness, except for the rooks circling noisily overhead. In the silence of the frozen morning, high overhead a robin thrills out its melodious song.

The pigeon's swirling flight makes it an awkward target and illustrates why true winter sporting guns prefer to test their skill with this bird rather than the cumbersome pheasant. Its rural name is the 'ringed dove', which refers to the distinctive white markings on the neck and wings. The soft '*coo*' of the wood pigeon has a soothing and sleepy sound during spring and summer days, but it belies the damage these birds can cause to crops. There is an old Wessex rhyme:

*Sow four beans as you make your row,*
*One for to rot and one to grow,*
*And one for the pigeon and one for the crow*

In spring a flock of pigeons can decimate a field of newly sown crops. A single pigeon eats a large handful of grain or seedlings a day and, as we have seen, a flock of 1,000 birds can strip acres of arable land in a day. The bird is a late nester and produces two broods just as the harvest is ripening. The young chicks are known as squabs and are fed on 'pigeon milk', a cheesy-like substance rich in protein, which the parents regurgitate from the crop. It is the only bird to produce milk similar to that of mammals. Pigeons are best eaten young but older birds can be used in casseroles and stews.

## RECIPE: Pigeon Casserole

*2 oz butter*
*3 slices lean bacon, chopped*
*8 spring onions, trimmed and chopped*
*8 oz button mushrooms, wiped clean and halved*
*breasts from four pigeons*
*1 pint water*
*4 teaspoons tomato purée*
*grated rind of lemon*

In a large frying pan, melt the butter and when the foam subsides add the bacon and spring onions and cook until the bacon is lightly browned. Remove from the pan and place in a large oven-proof casserole. Place the pigeon breasts in the frying pan and cook them, turning frequently until they are lightly browned. Transfer to the casserole. Add the mushrooms to the pan and cook for about 3 mins or until they are well coated with butter. Tip the contents of the pan over the meat. Return the pan to the heat, pour in the water and stir in the tomato purée and lemon rind. When the liquid boils, remove the pan from the heat and pour contents into the casserole. Cover and place in the oven for 1 hour or until the breasts are tender when pierced with the point of a sharp knife (350 F, 180 C, Gas Mark 4). Remove the casserole from the oven and serve immediately with mashed potatoes and steamed French beans.

In the farmhouse kitchen, the pantry will be stocked with all kinds of pickles and preserves made during the autumn. This is the time for entertaining family and friends and creating a homely atmosphere of warmth and hospitality. If we want to be really traditional, we can stretch the celebrations from the old Roman festival of Saturnalia on the 17th December until Twelfth Night on the 6th January when old Yule coincided with the Julian calendar.

One of the old ways of observing the Yule celebration to welcome back the sun-king was the burning of an ash faggott, made up of ash twigs, to be burned at the Winter Solstice to ensure good fortune. A miniature one can also be kept in the house for good luck. Everyone's attention will be on the coming festivities, just as they have been for thousands of years – when people waited for the 'longest night' to herald the approaching spring. Next to the traditional Harvest Home, perhaps Yule is the second most important festival in the calendar of the countryman, although Yule, i.e. Christmas, tends to be a far grander celebration.

## Suggestions for a traditional Yule Dinner

**First Course:**

Scotch broth, kidney soup, hare soup, cream of green peas, onion, potato or artichoke soup, or hors d'oeuvres, sardines, liver sausage, potato salad and beetroot.

**Second Course:**

Roast beef, pork, chicken, duck, goose or cottage goose (rolled, stuffed pork), turkey or stuffed breast of lamb.

**Accompaniments:**

Baked potatoes, buttered peas or Brussels sprouts. Serve bread sauce  with chicken or turkey and apple sauce with duck, pork or goose,  and fried rolls of bacon, or small sausages with any bird.

**Third Course:**

Plum pudding and custard sauce, flavoured with rum or brandy, and mince pies.

**Dessert:**

Oranges, bananas, dates, figs and nuts.

With wild boar now back in fashion, it can make a welcome change from that American import – the turkey. Wild boar was used for more than 1,000 years to mark the festive season in this country and the boar's head with an apple in its mouth dates back to the Norse Yule pig sacrifice at the turn of the year. The boar was sacred to both the Celt and Norse peoples, who believed that its flesh was the food of the heroes of Valhalla.

The ceremony of the Boar's Head is still observed in Queen's College, Oxford, as it has been since 1341, on the last Saturday before Christmas. The head decorated with sprigs of rosemary, holly and bay, with an orange in its mouth, is presented to the Provost and Fellows at the High Table, while the choir sings *The Boar's Head Carol*...

*The bores hed in handis I brynge*

*With garlands gay and birdis syngynge*
*I pray you all helpe me to synge*
*Que estis inconvinio.*

And for those who overindulge, there is the traditional pick-me-up that is also a comfort drink given to invalids – the posset.

## RECIPE: A Calming Yule Posset

*1 pint milk*
*6 fl ozs white wine*
*2 oz brown sugar*
*1 lemon*
*1 teaspoon ground or fresh ginger*
*Grating of nutmeg*

Boil the milk, pour in the wine and let the mixture cool until it curdles. Strain off the curds, add the sugar, the whole lemon and spices. Serve like yoghurt.

**An extract from *A Treasury of the Countryside*, published in 2003**

This extract contains all the traditional ingredients for an old-fashioned Yuletide celebration with plenty of history, wildlife, folk customs, nostalgia and hearty recipes. Although it wouldn't stand alone as an article for a country magazine, it could be broken down into mini-facts and submitted to half a dozen different magazines.

## Marketplace
**Wildlife publications have a wide readership that often has little connection with country living but they can provide yet another marketplace [*BBC Wildlife Magazine*, *Irish Wildlife Magazine*, *Canadian Wildlife Magazine*, *National Wildlife***

*Magazine* **(USA),** *Wildlife Australia Magazine*].

Ever since Bill Oddie introduced the world to *Springwatch*, people have become fascinated by the private life of birds and mammals; and perhaps the opposition to the proposed badger cull wouldn't have been so fierce if folk hadn't become so well acquainted with the daily doings of Mr and Mrs Brock and all their little Brocks. The public has become obsessed with wildlife, as the growing number of wildlife publications will show, and the market grows even wider for country writers.

Needless to say, the writer needs to be fully aware of the editorial parameters and politics of each individual publication to avoid giving offence by writing about taboo subjects such as culling, trapping, hunting, etc., and avoiding sentimentality at all costs. Here market research is just as important, so study your target publications and see how the other contributors submit their material. Which 'causes' are supported by the editor?

There is also room for wildlife pieces in the country magazines, particularly those like *The Countryman*; while *The Shooting Times* and *Countryman's Weekly* will accept wildlife articles on game and its conservation. There have been many articles written on the famous Connemara stags, for example, and no reader could fail to be impressed by these awesome animals no matter how they view wildlife.

## Exercise: Mini-Facts and Fillers

Mini-articles or 'fillers' are usually how-to pieces that all editors need throughout the year to fill odd corners of the magazine. These range from contributions to the Letters page to 500-word fillers – usually related to seasonal topics or referring to articles previously published. The online how-to site Howopia under the 'Sports & Fitness' category accepted the following how-to piece...

## How To Arrange A 'Car Boot' Picnic

Anyone who has ever been to a game or agricultural fair, point-to-point meeting, or any other form of rural sporting event, will know the importance of providing a 'good boot'. This is an informal picnic served from the boot of the car – although serving is the only informal thing about it, because there is usually a tremendous amount of preparation involved in the variety and amount of food provided.

## What you'll need

1 dozen mugs
6 whiskey tumblers
6 each knives and teaspoons
1 dozen tea towels
Large picnic basket or hamper
A selection of different sized plastic storage containers
Hot water jugs or a camping kettle
Plenty of napkins

- The experienced rural hostess knows to take plenty of food in order to feed the many 'strays' that turn up uninvited, and there's never a risk of throwing anything away.
- A typical countryman's boot would be expected to offer soup (home-made or good quality tinned – not soup-in-a-mug variety); hot sausages; sausage rolls; hard-boiled eggs; cold chicken; game, egg and bacon, or veal and ham pie; a large selection of sandwiches/rolls with substantial fillings of roast meat or ham; plain rolls and butter, cheese, and large slabs of fruit cake.
- Pack the food, especially cake, sandwiches and rolls, in large plastic storage containers to prevent it from getting squashed. Keep the soup and sausages hot in airtight thermos food jugs. Offer food straight from the container to be eaten with the fingers – plates are not necessary.

- Coffee should be made at the boot as required rather than taken ready prepared – a camping kettle keeps the water boiling – and should be available all day to keep out the cold, often being liberally laced with whisk(e)y. Hot whiskey and sloe gin is another favourite tipple against the bitter cold.
- Wine is best left to warmer pursuits as chilled Chardonnay can paralyse the bladder, while vintage red brought to impress the guests can taste like paint-stripper when served in an icy wind in the middle of an open field.
- Don't be too keen to pack up and close the boot until your neighbours do, even if you're frozen to the bone. A lot of socialising goes on after the event has finished while allowing for traffic to clear.

## Conclusion:

If you're new to this sort of thing, accept any invitations to see how other people run their boot but don't be a 'guest' too often before reciprocating or you'll be looked upon as a free-loader. At these events people do the rounds, so expect to cater for more folk than you actually know. Keep some of the picnic back for a second serving and avoid the embarrassment of running out of food. A well-run boot is part of the social routine at most rural winter sporting events, and can even be found at more urban gatherings such as Twickenham and Goodwood.

Tips:

- Take plenty of tea towels for packing and drying up.
- Don't forget mustard, milk, sugar, pepper and salt.
- People eat with their fingers, so plenty of napkins should be available. Paper is fine, linen is better.
- Don't be snobbish. Offer food and drink to the help, not just the participants.

Warnings:

- If you really want to blend in, don't use a new picnic set with quilted inside and neatly stacking plates and cutlery. Invest in a large battered wicker basket or hamper, and wrap everything in clean, linen tea towels!
- A heavy wax coat and hat with Dubarry boots are the dress code of the day. Few people look elegant on the rural sporting field and warmth is the first priority.

Not really a sports how-to on the surface but there are lots of sporting occasions where a car boot picnic can come in useful – usually because on-site catering is generally so appalling and expensive. If you watch carefully, you'll find similar arrangements at events such as Silverstone, Ascot and Clonmel where the picnic served from the back of the car is viewed as part of the day's enjoyment.

# Once In A Blue Moon

A 'blue moon' is something that occurs rarely – but don't write about it, because hundreds of others will have already done so – and submitting their piece to the same magazines that you wish to target. The perennial writers' favourites of badgers and blue tits, seedtime and harvest are probably as tedious to the readers as they are to the editor, so look for a new slant on popular topics.

## Originality

As we observed in the first chapter (January: The Dark Month), it is not easy to be original – as previously noted, even the philosophers tell us that there is no such thing as original thought. All editors, however, are looking for an element of action, drama or surprise, even in non-fiction. It's what catches their attention and makes them pause to read further; and the key to any editor's heart is originality. Not necessarily a new departure in style or genre, but a refreshing and original slant on a popular theme.

The writers whose work has been accepted for publication managed to spark the editor's interest because those particular typescripts stood out from the rest on a dull, wet Monday morning. It's not always easy to be objective about our own work, but the first question we need to ask is: why did those other writers stand out? What was so special about one of those particular pieces of writing? What made the editor decide to publish it over the hundreds of others (including our own submission) arriving in the office during that month?

- It may have been brilliantly written – but so are hundreds of others.
- It was probably topical – but so are hundreds of others.

- It probably met every point in the contributors' guidelines – but so did hundreds of others.

The answer, without doubt, was that particular writer's approach to a common or popular theme was so fresh and appealing that it was almost as if the editor was reading about the subject for the first time. In other words – **originality!**

One of the first instructions I usually give at a writers' workshop is to always discard the first idea that comes into your head. And while you're at it, discard the second... and third idea, too. This is because a hundred other writers will have had an identical thought for an article (poem or short story) stimulated by something seen on television, read in a magazine or newspaper, or heard on the radio. We may not *consciously* realise that this has been the source of our inspiration but the seed has been planted firmly in the deep recesses of the brain.

So the next time you have an idea, stop and ask yourself: "How obvious is this approach?" and "How can I make it different?"

## Life As It Is Lived: The Reality

It was a glorious summer's day when the agent brought us to see Gurtavoher House. A very grand name for a very small cottage, complete with stables and barn, but it was south-facing, tucked into the side of a steep ridge, and with spectacular views of the Galtee Mountains. This sheltered location, we were assured, was guaranteed to avoid much of the watery depression that normally sweeps inland over Tipperary from the Atlantic.

It is the sort of traditional family property that native-born Irish offload as quickly as possible in adulthood, in favour of a new-build, all mod cons bungalow. There is also the traditional pervading dampness that can only be rectified by continuously feeding the huge solid fuel Stanley cooker summer and winter. Nevertheless, we were blinded by the romance of two-foot thick stone walls, open fireplaces and a reasonable rent for a small-holding in the heart of Ireland's hunting country. Surrounded by lush vegetation it was a testament to the Glen's more temperate climate, which is always a few degrees milder than on the other side of the ridge.

Rain is a way of life in Ireland. Air arriving on Kerry's shores has crossed the ocean, where it has acquired large quantities of moisture, which is duly deposited in Munster. From fine drizzle to stair-rods, water not only comes down, it also comes up. Within a week of moving into our rural paradise, the weather had returned to normal and the bathroom wall sprouted a curious growth of mould that could only be eradicated by leaving the windows open in all weathers and liberal applications of Jeyes Fluid.

There was also an interesting water feature in the kitchen, complete with a hideous fungus that looked suspiciously like one of those marked with a skull and crossbones in *Mushrooms and Toadstools of Britain and Europe*. The problem was identified as a fractured perforation drainage pipe that had been laid to deflect water coming off the ridge behind the cottage into the stream. An overenthusiastic digger driver had crushed the pipe during the renovations and so a yawning trench had to be dug to accommodate a new one. Within minutes the carefully raked drive gravel was a sea of wet clay as the machine clawed at the earth – ripping up the mains water pipe in the process.

Even during the summer months, the Irish working day is short and by four o'clock it was all over. We still had water on the kitchen floor but none in the pipes. Fortunately, both being veterans of French holiday campaigns, we managed to straddle the open manhole (the cover being concealed somewhere under piles of wet clay), followed up by a bucket of water from the stream. This delicate manoeuvre had to be carried out when our neighbouring farmer wasn't attending to his cattle, otherwise our initial introduction would have been as pale, squatting rear ends visible through the dividing greenery and driving rain.

The first wave of workmen arrived at nine o'clock the following morning, whereupon they demanded tea and settled down in the van to consume large quantities of sandwiches, and the entire contents of the Irish *Mirror*, having only left home some 15 minutes previously. The second wave arrived an hour later and more tea was provided. The rain continued to fall, and after much teeth sucking, it was decided to replace the pipes under the entrance to the property, to allow the stream greater egress. By midday there was a seven-foot deep trench, which is when disaster struck again.

The digger broke down. It was Friday lunchtime when, in true Irish building trade tradition, everyone knocks off for the weekend. Numerous increasingly hysterical telephone calls were made until the 'hose doctor' turned up at three o'clock to carry out the necessary hydraulic repairs. By this time things were well behind schedule for knocking off, but there was no escape since all the vehicles were on the *wrong* side of the steep, water-filled trench.

'imself whistling *How Do You Like Your Eggs In The Morning?* only added to the mounting desperation of men who were losing valuable drinking time and crumbling under the strain. By late afternoon the huge concrete pipes were in place, with rocks and other debris flung on top to replace the drive. The garden and paddock resembled the Somme as workmen, clinging to whatever foot and handhold they could find on the wagon, were last seen disappearing down the *boreen* in true Keystone Kops fashion.

There was a brief, unspoken debate of who was to use the bathroom first and I lost. Following hurried footsteps on the floor above, the silence was broken by a welcome flushing noise... and then the pipe to the lavatory exploded!

The above is the proposed opening for a non-fiction book on

country living – a sort of blending of 'A Year in the Glen' (with apologies to Peter Mayle) and *Any Fool's* Country Life by James Robertson. *Signposts For Country Living* was intended as a step-by-step guide to finding a property, settling down, becoming part of the community and avoiding the pitfalls often experienced by the 'incomer' and stressing the point that blundering about and trusting to luck won't help at all. *The Country Writer's Craft* is a blend of my own knowledge of country-lore and over 20 years of creative writing publishing, editing and tutorials, which hopefully will show others how to make a successful writing career in writing for country, regional and rural publications.

## Marketplace

**Specialist book publishers who accept full-length typescripts on all aspects of country living [The Good Life Press, Countryside Books, Merlin Unwin Books, Quiller Publishing, Shire Books, Country Books etc.]**

Sooner or later writers will want to try their hand at writing a full-length book on country experiences and ours was *Signposts For Country Living*, published by **The Good Life Press** in 2010. **Country Books** (www.countrybooks.biz) specialise in local histories and have recently released a new 'ghost walks' series; seeing that Britain has more ghosts than anywhere else in the world, it might provide an interesting opportunity. Submit ideas in the form of a synopsis in the first instance.

**Shire Books** (www.shirebooks.co.uk) also offers a particularly interesting opportunity as they specialise in 'small books on all manner of obscure subjects' and according to the guidelines: "You don't have to live in the country to write books for Shire but it helps." Many of the publications are slim paperbacks similar to a title I have on my reference shelf – *Discovering Horse Brasses*, which is only 48 pages – and the titles list includes categories such as rural history and bygones, canals and waterways, walking books, folklore and local history. Check the website for more information.

The best places to locate publishers of country topics, however, are the reviews and advertisement sections found in the different publications catering for rural interests. Publishers in this genre are usually small, independent houses and don't widely feature in the writers' handbooks; once we start digging, we find there are lots more outlets than we think.

## Exercise: Another Word of Warning

Action Man's been at it again… whilst commiserating with a local farmer's wife over the state of British farming, she just happened to mention that the person currently engaged in writing the history of the village was having to stop due to age and infirmity – *he* just happened to mention he knew someone who might be able to help!

Local histories are extremely emotive and often lend themselves to full-scale warfare before the typescript gets to the printers, so it's not somewhere that *un o bant,* or a 'stranger' as we say in Wales, should rush gamely towards. The main problem is sorting out the priorities and everyone concerned has their own idea about what is, and what is not, important. Old village families often look on the project as their own personal history, while incomers are not usually privy to the local legends, gossip and folklore so necessary to spice up the text

The whole point of any publishing project is to a) produce a book with the widest possible reader appeal, which stands more chance of b) making it financially viable. A good cause to which any profits can be donated is usually a strong selling point but how does one choose between the church restoration fund, the cricket club and the WI? And in hunting country with history and society firmly rooted in the hunting tradition, how much emphasis can be placed on this without alienating other would-be purchasers?

So, before getting to the first fence, there's enough village politics stirred up to keep feelings running high for months and there hasn't even been a preliminary meeting to discuss tactics and approach. Those born and bred in the rural Britain know that village feuds can instil shivers of dread in the most hardened of countrymen.

Should anyone be tempted to traverse this potential minefield, I would suggest that two forms of attack be implemented before anything else is agreed upon. Firstly, as a professional writer you retain the right to veto any contributions that fail to compliment the text; and secondly, that the local artist does *not* provide the cover illustration – unless they just happen to be brilliant which is rare indeed. There's many a self-published book that's been totally ruined simply because no one dare say 'no' to the husband's brother's wife's artwork for fear of giving offence.

Make sure you've asked all the right questions *before* agreeing to take on the job and, more importantly, try to ascertain just how much information there is actually available and who is going to provide it. Even if you decide to take on the job without payment, this does not excuse any lack of professionalism in your approach. It will be your responsibility to provide the best 'service' you can give; after all, it's your by-line on the cover even if you're not being paid for it!

**Published in the November 2000 issue of** *The New Writer*

## Closing ...

Remember that as writers, we are painting a portrait of country living that often encourages town people to make the move, and we have a responsibility to create our pictures as a true representative of what rural life is really like. In more isolated areas the houses may have no mains gas or drainage, which means relying on bottled gas and the vagaries of a septic tank or cesspit. It may even be necessary to cart the weekly rubbish some distance to the nearest pickup point.

Public transport is often next to non-existent with hospitals, sports facilities and schools miles away. When there is only one family car then shopping may be restricted to the village shop or garage, which can be expensive, although Internet shopping with the larger supermarkets is now popular in rural areas for precisely this reason. Emergency services will take much longer to arrive because they usually have to cover a wider area. Our social life will always involve travelling some distance for the theatre and cinema, and in the more rural areas much of the social activity revolves around traditional country activities and sports.

We are also conscious that many smaller villages in remote areas are dying. Young local people cannot afford the house prices that have escalated way beyond their means, and so many of them have been forced to move away. The lack of young families means there is often now no need for the village school and, with diminishing amenities such as a general store and/or Post Office, the village becomes a 'dormitory' with hardly any signs of life during the day.

The responsible writer must also record the downside of a rural lifestyle; but at the end of the day, isn't doesn't stop us from living here – loving where we live – and writing about it.

**COMPASS
BOOKS**

Compass Books focuses on practical and informative 'how-to' books for writers. Written by experienced authors who also have extensive experience of tutoring at the most popular creative writing workshops, the books offer an insight into the more specialised niches of the publishing game.